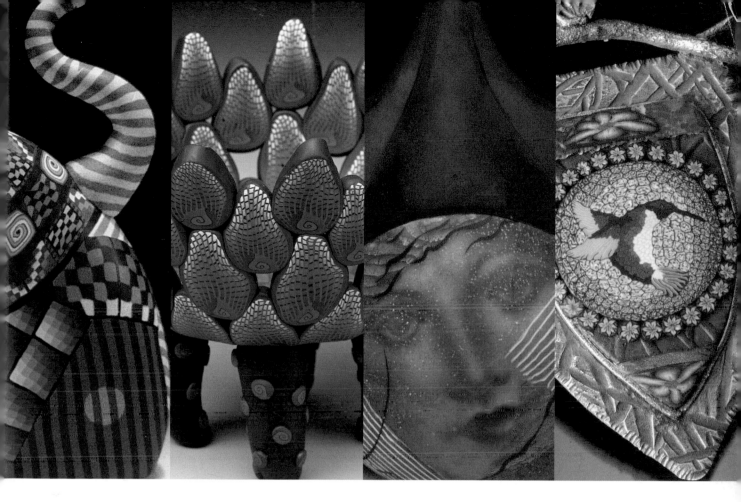

400 POLYMER CLAY DESIGNS

A COLLECTION OF DYNAMIC & COLORFUL CONTEMPORARY WORK

400 POLYMER CLAY DESIGNS

A COLLECTION OF DYNAMIC & COLORFUL CONTEMPORARY WORK

INTRODUCTION BY IRENE SEMANCHUK DEAN

LARK BOOKS

A Division of Sterling Publishing Co., Inc.
New York

Editor: **Suzanne J. E. Tourtillott**
Art Director: **828, Inc.**
Cover Designer: **Barbara Zaretsky**
Assistant Editor: **Nathalie Mornu**
Associate Art Director: **Shannon Yokeley**
Art Intern: **Sharease Curl**
Editorial Assistance: **Delores Gosnell, Rosemary Kast, Jeff Hamilton**
Editorial Intern: **Kalin E. Siegwald**

Cover Images: Cover, Harriet Smith, *Heart Box*, 2002, photo by Eugenia Uhl; **front flap**, Jeffrey Lloyd Dever, *Stickpins–Nature Form Trio*, 2003, photo by Gregory R. Staley; **spine**, Cynthia Pack, *Petal Bowl*, 2002, photo by Steve Mann; **back cover** (left), Sandra McCaw, *Winter Bloom*, 2002, photo by Jeff Baird; **back cover** (center top), Bonnie Bishoff and J.M. Syron, *Star Chair*, 2002, photo by Dean Powell; **back cover** (center bottom), Cynthia Toops and Chuck Domitrovich (jewelry), *The Bird*, 2003, photo by Roger Schreiber; **back flap**, Andrée Chénier, *Elf of the Court #1*, 2003, photo by Steve Mann

Library of Congress Cataloging-in-Publication Data

Tourtillott, Suzanne J. E.
  400 polymer clay designs : a collection of dyamic & colorful contemporary work / Suzanne J.E. Tourtillott.
       p. cm.
   ISBN 1-57990-460-2 (pbk.)
    1. Polymer clay craft. I. Title.
   TT297.T68 2004
   731.4'2--dc22

                               2003026975

10 9 8 7 6 5 4 3

Published by Lark Books, A Division of
Sterling Publishing Co., Inc.
387 Park Avenue South, New York, N.Y. 10016

© 2004, Lark Books

Distributed in Canada by Sterling Publishing,
c/o Canadian Manda Group, 165 Dufferin Street
Toronto, Ontario, Canada M6K 3H6

Distributed in the U.K. by Guild of Master Craftsman Publications Ltd.,
Castle Place, 166 High Street, Lewes, East Sussex, England BN7 1XU
Tel: (+ 44) 1273 477374, Fax: (+ 44) 1273 478606,
Email: pubs@thegmcgroup.com, Web: www.gmcpublications.com

Distributed in Australia by Capricorn Link (Australia) Pty Ltd.,
P.O. Box 704, Windsor, NSW 2756 Australia

If you have questions or comments about this book, please contact:
Lark Books
67 Broadway
Asheville, NC 28801
(828) 253-0467

Manufactured in China

ISBN 1-57990-460-2

C O N T E N T S

INTRODUCTION

The images presented in *400 Polymer Clay Designs* make up perhaps the largest collection of polymer clay creations ever published. Originally this pliable polymer material was developed in Germany for dollmakers and miniaturists, but over the years it's grown well beyond its initial purpose. Here you'll indeed find dolls and figurines (both realistic and fanciful), but there are also many beautiful pieces of jewelry and beads, decorative boxes, wall pieces, finely crafted purses and furniture—in short, a myriad of *objets d'art*.

As I reviewed the hundreds of slides that were submitted by artists from all over the world, I marveled at the growth of polymer clay as an artistic medium. In many respects it's the perfect kind of forming material for creative expression: it comes in an unbelievable range of colors, is widely available (and relatively inexpensive), and is capable of being both infinitely malleable and, after having been cured, quite reliably permanent. Polymer clay is popular with accomplished artists and novices alike because of these unique working properties.

In the early- to mid-1970s, a handful of artists began experimenting with polymer clay to make jewelry, sculptural vessels, and more. Some of these pioneers, such as Kathleen Dustin, Pier Volkous, Kathy Amt, Tory Hughes, and Steven Ford and David Forlano (City Zen Cane), showed this material to their fellow artists or taught classes, and the enthusiasm for polymer clay snowballed. Within 10 to 15 years, polymer clay had become the medium of choice for many established artists and inventive amateurs. In the last decade alone, their skill and vision have pressed manufacturers to expand the versatility of polymer clay. There are now clays that are translucent, metallic, and, remarkably, even liquid. In turn these new qualities have enabled artists to explore and master new intricacies in caneworking, faux surfaces, and transfer imagery—all methods that are shared in other artistic media as well.

The amount of time that polymer clay has been used as an expressive medium is a mere blip on the artistic timeline—think about how long fiber, dyes, earthen clay, and glass have been around. Compared to other media, polymer clay is still in its infancy. Already in its short lifetime we've witnessed an amazing increase in the amount of resources available to us. There are tools made specifically for this material, as well as numerous books, videos, and classes focusing on polymer clay. The National Polymer Clay Guild has given rise to many regional guilds, and countless websites are devoted to the medium. Today, as a material that is capable of great transformation, polymer clay is increasingly pressed into the service of multi-media work. Here you'll find many works that feature metal, wood, found objects, and fabric. No doubt that by the time this book reaches your hands, new techniques will have been developed and spread through the polymer clay community.

My own journey with polymer clay began when I happened on Nan Roche's landmark *The New Clay*, which showcased work from many of those pioneers. The first beads I made, from a simple green and pearl-white jellyroll cane, addicted me. I was intrigued by the technique and excited by the immediacy of this material. My work has evolved and matured in the years since I first made those green and white beads, yet, as I share with and learn from others, I continue to be awed by the infinite potential of polymer clay. I share some of those awe-inspiring possibilities with you here in this volume.

The 400 polymer clay creations presented in this book showcase a wide spectrum of styles and techniques. Occasionally I was moved to comment on some aspect of an object's artistry, and sometimes the artists themselves shared the inspiration, observations, and challenges they met in the process of creating the work. Pieces range in size from Kim Matthews' detailed miniature fruit-and-cheese platter to J. M. Syron's and Bonnie Bishoff's remarkable veneers on fine furniture. Rachel Gourley's highly textural sculpture and Virginia Sperry's intricately caneworked self-portrait are outstanding examples of decorative surfaces. Included are pieces from some of the masters of this medium, whose distinctive styles and consistent creativity are instantly recognizable in the polymer clay community. Some pieces are from artists who have come to polymer clay from other media and bring fresh perspectives to the medium. Still other pieces are from promising new creators who are finding their voices—some for the first time—with polymer clay. It is my pleasure and honor to bring these pieces together in one collection.

Irene Semanchuk Dean

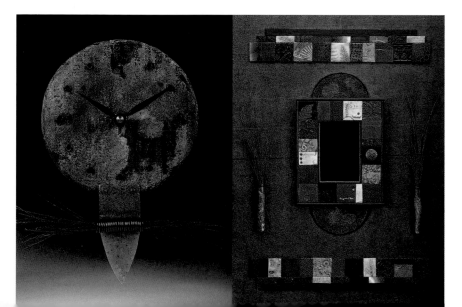

IRENE SEMANCHUK DEAN

(Left)
Clock, 2003
5 x 8" (12.7 x 20.3 cm)
Premo!; twigs, CD, acrylic paint, clock mechanism; stamped, antiqued
Photo by Stewart Stokes

(Right)
Wall Piece with Mirror, 2003
18 x 24" (45.7 x 61 cm)
Premo!; mirror, CDs, plywood, test tubes, twigs, found objects, acrylic and spray paints; textured, stamped, mokume gane
Photo by Stewart Stokes

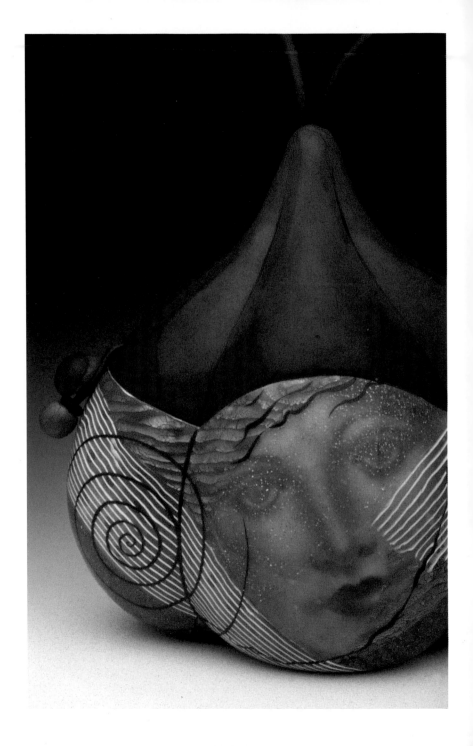

KATHLEEN DUSTIN

Squash-Shaped Bracelet Purse, 2002
7 x 6 x 4" (17.5 x 15.2 x 10.2 cm)
Premo!, Sculpey III, liquid polymer; colored
pencil, gold leaf, Viton rubber handle;
multiple layering and baking, sanded,
polished
Photo by George Post

I use the vehicle of evening purses
because I want people to appreciate my
work intimately, not just from a distance.
Instead of just looking at it on a shelf, I
encourage them to look at it closely, touch
it often, and even bring it with them. –KD

Kathleen Dustin's flawless work has an
otherworldly, ethereal aspect and is
influenced by her travels and her interest
in the female face and form. –ISD

GERRI NEWFRY

Artist's Box, 2002
3 ¾ x 4 ¼ x 3 ¾" (9.4 x 10.8 x 9.4 cm)
Premo!; acrylic, acrylic wash; millefiori, rubber stamped
Photo by Larry Sanders

DEBORAH ANDERSON

Purse-ibilities, 2002
20" (50.8 cm)
Fimo; canework
Photo by Liv Ames

KARYN KOZAK

Bug, 2002
2" (5.1 cm)
Fimo; telephone wire, silver wire, glass bead,
interference powders; millefiori
Photo by Ryell Ho

I began doing bugs in October, 1999. I needed a
Halloween costume and used my initials as
inspiration. I made about 20 crawlies and came as
2K Bugged. –*KK*

Tiny details and a precise arrangement of color,
texture, and pattern make Karyn Kozak's insect pins
fascinating to examine. –*ISD*

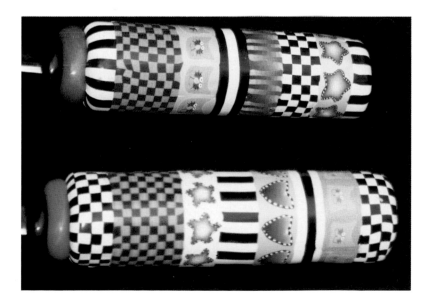

KAREN SCUDDER

Untitled, 2002
2 x 9 x 1" (5.1 x 22.9 x 2.5 cm)
Premo!; stainless steel utensils
Photo by artist

TERI BYRD

Luther's Down Time, 2002
4 ½ x 3 x 4 ½" (11.4 x 7.5 x 11.4 cm)
Premo!; wire and foil armature, paint; canework
Photo by Rober Batey

Luther is one figure from my Americana series,
which is based on people and activities I've
observed and fondly remember. –TB

CHRISTOPHER KNOPPEL

Face of Domestic & Sexual Violence, 2002
7 x 5 x 3" (17.5 x 12.7 x 7.5 cm)
Fimo, Translucent Liquid Sculpey; aluminum
contour mesh wire, eggshells, acrylic paints,
silver leaf, paper, wood board; rubber stamped
Photo by artist

This wall piece was made for an invitational
exhibition called *Artful Sentiments*, which
benefited the Oregon Coalition Against
Domestic and Sexual Violence. –CK

ARLENE SUMMERS

Colette, 2002
17 x 5 x 5" (43.2 x 12.7 x 12.7 cm)
Fimo; ribbon, net, sequins, Tibetan lambswool,
glass beads, cabochon, wire
Photo by Jeff Demian

Colette is a magnificent mime inspired by the
age-old circus/theatre tradition of characters
like Harlequin, Columbine, and Pierrot. –AS

MARAH ANDERSON

Maryjanes With Flowers, 2001
1 ½ x 2 x 4 ½" (3.8 x 5.1 x 11.3 cm)
Fimo; canework
Photo by Liv Ames

SYBILLE HAMILTON

Pod Bracelet, 2002
1 x 3 ¾ x 2 ½" (2.5 x 9.4 x 6.3 cm)
Polymer clay; acrylic paint
Photo by Laura Timmins

CHRIS BIVINS

Olive Cat, 2002
12 x 10 x 2" (30.5 x 25.4 x 5.1 cm)
Sculpey; feathers, copper wire, fabric, wood
Photo by Gary Darby

I like making these dolls because of the variety
of materials I get to use. I have an incredibly
short attention span, but the versatility of
polymer clay keeps me interested and it works
well with other materials. –CB

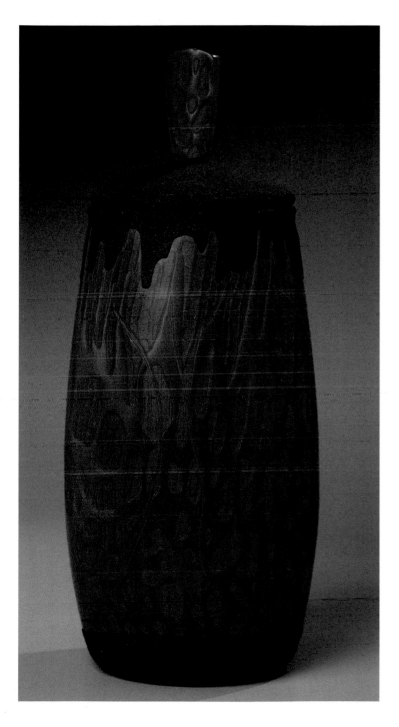

GRANT DIFFENDAFFER

Red Jar, 2003
10 ½ x 4 ½ x 4 ½" (26.7 x 11.4 x 11.4 cm)
Premo!; glass; mokume gane, texturized
Photo by Kim Harrington

I create pieces inspired by natural patterns seen
through the lenses of microscopes, telescopes,
and dive masks. *–GD*

CATHERINE VERDIERE

Aquatique, 2003
14 ¼" (36 cm); pendant 3 ¼ x 1 ⅛" (8.5 x 3 cm)
Polymer clay; metal parts, silver wire
Photo by Philippe Deneufve

TEJAE HALL

1 ⅜" Mini Pink Heart Box, 2003
¹¹⁄₁₆ x 1 ⅜ x 1 ⅛" (1.7 x 3.5 x 2.9 cm)
Sculpey III
Photo by Casey Chinn Photography

Sometimes happy accidents create successful pieces. −TH

PEG GERARD

Mimbres Warrior & Deer Necklace, 1998
3 x 2 x 1" (7.5 x 5.1 x 2.5 cm)
Fimo; metallic foil; canework
Photo by Pat Berrett

KLEW [KAREN LEWIS]

Untitled, 2000
30" (76.2 cm)
Polymer clay; sterling wire, semi-
precious beads
Photo by George Post

GWEN GIBSON

Africa, 2002
21" (53.3 cm) long
Premo!; PearlEx powder, friction clasp; press molded
Photo by Robert Diamante

RACHEL CARREN

Fresco Bracelet, 2002
1 ½ x 2 ½ x 2 ½" (3.8 x 6.3 x 6.3 cm)
Premo!
Photo by Ralph Gabriner

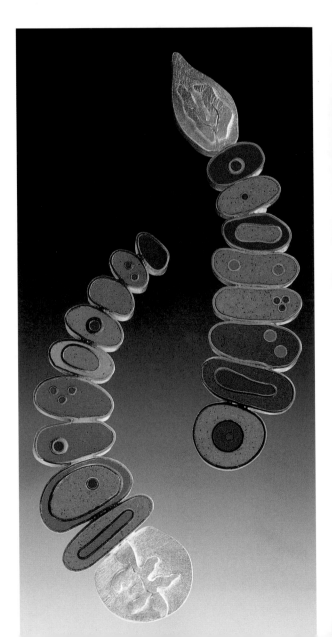

**MARY FILAPEK
LOU ANN TOWNSEND**

Taking Root (left); *Budding* (right), 2003
Each 3 x 1 ¼ x ³⁄₁₆" (7.5 x 3.2 x .5 cm)
Polymer clay; sterling silver
Photo by Margot Geist

CYNTHIA TOOPS

Peace Offering, 2002
3 ½ x 2 ½ x 1 ¼" (8.8 x 6.3 x 3.2 cm)
Fimo, Sculpey III; micromosaic threads
Photo by Dan Adams

I usually employ polymer clay to create jewelry
work but once in a while, for a change of pace,
I challenge myself to make containers like this
small teapot. The hat acts as the lid and the spout
is at the shoulder. *—CT*

LORETTA ANNE CASTAGNA

Pinnate Series Pendant #2, 2000
2 x 1 ¼" (5 x 3 cm)
Polymer clay; sterling silver, freshwater pearl; nerikomi canework, fabricated
Photo by Allan Bryan

The Pinnate Series is a study in renewal and growth. Vibrant, dynamic polymer inlays enliven the sterling silver frames. The polymer is caned, but the cane is assembled at scale and never reduced— a technique more similar to Japanese nerikomi porcelain than millefiori glass. As a result the polymer retains clean, crisp lines reminiscent of the modern art of Wassily Kandinsky and Robert Delaunay. *–LAC*

JUDY S. BELCHER
KIP CHRISTENSEN

Tessellation in Black and White, 2002
7 ¾ x 1 ¼ x ¼" (19.7 x 3.2 x .6 cm)
Fimo; jet beads, sterling silver spacer beads and clasp; millefiori
Photo by Steve Payne

Each of the beads in this bracelet is made from one cane, sliced and tessellated into all these different patterns. To think—one cane, millions of possibilities. *–JSB*

DEBBIE KRUEGER

Charm Necklace, 2002
24" (61 cm)
Polymer clay, Precious Metal Clay;
sterling silver wire, glass beads;
canework, soldered, hammered
Photo by George Post

25

TAMELA WELLS LAITY

Necklace, 2003
22" (55.9 cm)
Premo!, Sculpey, Precious Metal Clay;
sterling beads, silver leaf
Photo by Tim Barnwell

LINDA LUBÉ

Awaken, 2001
12 x 10 x 1" (30.5 x 25.4 x 2.5 cm)
Premo!; handmade papers, acrylic
paints, Swarovski crystal, wire; textured

This series of artwork is subtitled
Messages for Planet Earth. This
piece is one of the wakeup calls I
make for myself, a nudge to come
out of a deep sleep. *–LL*

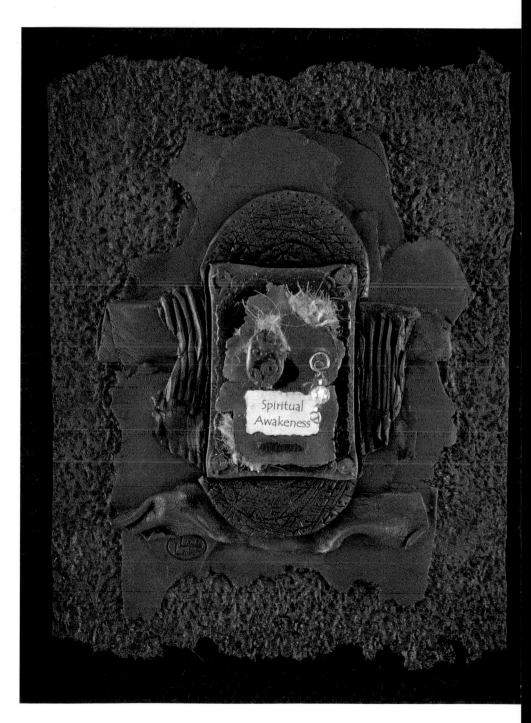

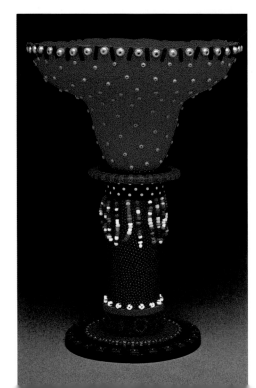

ANGIE WIGGINS

A Rose is Just a Rose, But a Margarita...Well..., 2003
7 ½ x 22 x 4 ¼" (19 x 55.9 x 10.8 cm)
Polymer clay; handmade paper, metallic powders,
ribbon, glass beads, leather, metal, wood, clay bead;
laminated, stamped
Photo by Taylor Dabney

I don't drink, but I think that the form of a margarita
glass is so beautiful. *—AW*

TERI BYRD

Underneath It All, 2003
4 ¼ x 2 ¾ x 1 ½" (10.8 x 7 x 3.8 cm)
Premo!; paint; canework
Photo by Robert Batey

Peeling away her frenetic exterior, she
reveals her more serene self. —TB

MARYANNE OLDENBURG

The Magic Orb, 2003
10 x 8 x 5" (25.4 x 20.3 x 12.7 cm)
Polymer clay; fabric, mohair wig, wood base
Photo by artist

CHRISTINE HARRIS

Dreaming, 2003
11 x 14 x 1 ½" (27.9 x 35.6 x 3.8 cm)
Sculpey III; wood, bottles, seeds, shells, jewelry
findings, acrylic paints, metallic wax, paint;
impressed, rubber stamped, carved, polished
Photo by Ben Harris

JOYCE FRITZ

Dragonfly Pin, 2003
2 ¼ x 2 x ⅛" (5.7 x 5.1 x .3 cm)
Fimo; glass beads, artistic wire
Photo by Larry Sanders

LINDA GOFF

This Old Byzantine Egg, 1999
5 x 7 x 5" (12.7 x 17.5 x 12.7 cm)
Polymer clay; ostrich egg, foils
Photo by Daniel S. Kapsner

GERRI NEWFRY

Madonna Journal (back), 2002
5 ¾ x 4 ½ x 1" (14.6 x 11.4 x 2.5 cm)
Premo!; silver leaf, waxed linen, archival
papers, acrylic, wire, chalk, ink; millefiori,
textured, rubber stamped
Photo by Larry Sanders

LOUISE FISCHER COZZI

Sophie Necklace, 2002
1 ½ x 16 ½ x 3 ³⁄₃₂" (1.3 x 41.9 x 7.7 cm)
Premo!; paint, pencil, leafing pen,
telephone wire, silver findings; bleached,
etched, painted
Photo by George Post

SYBILLE HAMILTON

Polymer Necklace, 2002
18 ³⁄₄" (48 cm); beads each approx.
⁵⁄₁₆ x ⁷⁄₁₆" (.8 x 1 cm)
Fimo; brass beads; mokume gane
Photo by Laura Timmins

KATHLEEN DUSTIN

Scream–Evening Purse, 2003
5 x 6 x 3 ½" (12.7 x 15.2 x 8.8 cm)
Premo!, Sculpey III, liquid polymer; colored pencil,
gold leaf, Viton rubber handle; multiple layering and
baking, sanded, polished
Photo by George Post

LAURA BALOMBINI

Dancer in the Dark, 2003
28 x 12 x 10" (71.1 x 30.5 x 25.4 cm)
Premo!; steel wire, oil paints
Photo by artist

LILIAN NICHOLS

Ribbon Necklace, 2002
8 ½ x 11 x 1" (21.6 x 27.9 x 2.5 cm)
Premo!
Photo by Russ Moore

CHRISTOPHER KNOPPEL

Emulsion Transfer Necklace, 2002
22" (55.9 cm)
Fimo, Translucent Liquid Sculpey; brass washers,
silver beads, seed beads, rubber cord, transferred
photographic emulsion
Photo by Don Felton

GRANT DIFFENDAFFER

Green Pendant, 2003
1 ¼ x 1 ¼ x ¼" (3.2 x 3.2 x .6 cm)
Premo!; rubber cord
Photo by Kim Harrington

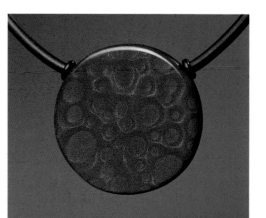

CHRIS BIVINS

Red Confetti Necklace, 2002
8 x 8 x ¼" (20.3 x 20.3 x .6 cm)
Sculpey SuperFlex; copper wire
Photo by Gary Darby

KELLIE ROBINSON

Faux Turquoise Choker, 2002
1 ¼ x 1 x ¾" (3.2 x 2.5 x 1.9 cm)
Premo!, Translucent Liquid Sculpey; oil paint,
PearlEx powders, sterling silver beads,
reconstituted-amber beads
Photo by Frank Flavin

KRISTA WELLS

Gregarious Grenadier, 2001
13 x 9 x 4" (33 x 22.9 x 10.2 cm)
Premo!, Fimo; glass and clay beads, driftwood,
wire, feathers; canework, textured
Photo by Julian Beveridge

Krista Wells makes inventive use of mixed
media to create work that is brimming with
charm and whimsy; this piece is reminiscent
of one of Dr. Seuss's characters. *–ISD*

PAM WYNN

Beads to the Knees, 2002
18 x 12 x 12" (45.7 x 30.5 x 30.5 cm)
Polymer clay; wood table, copper wire, glass
and crystal beads; sanded, buffed, textured
Photo by Meredith Hartsfield

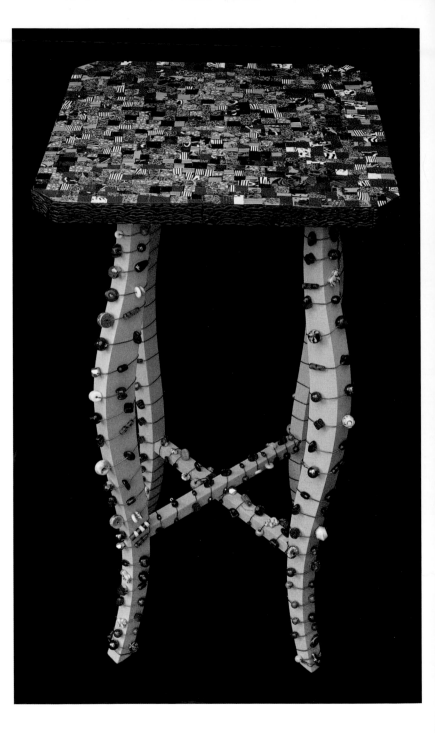

MAGS BONHAM

Spirit Boxes, 2002
Largest 3 x 3 x 3" (7.5 x 7.5 x 7.5 cm)
Premo!; glass beads, artistic wire
Photo by Jeff Clark

I start with a square sheet of clay and seal the edges together to trap the air inside the clay "envelope." The air heats up in the oven and creates the box's shape. *–MB*

LORETTA ANNE CASTAGNA

Pinnate Series Brooch #1, 2000
2 x 1 ¼" (5 x 3 cm)
Polymer clay; sterling silver, freshwater pearls;
nerikomi canework, fabricated
Photo by Allan Bryan

Polymer clay inlays are the focus of this clean,
asymmetrically balanced pendant, and the lines
of its pattern nicely harmonize with those of the
overall design. *–ISD*

DIANE VILLANO

Big Bead–Peruvian Ceramic Relic, 2002
3 ¾ x 3 ¾ x 3 ¾" (9.4 x 9.4 x 9.4 cm)
Premo!; wood, kumihimo cord, acrylic paint
Photo by William K. Sacco

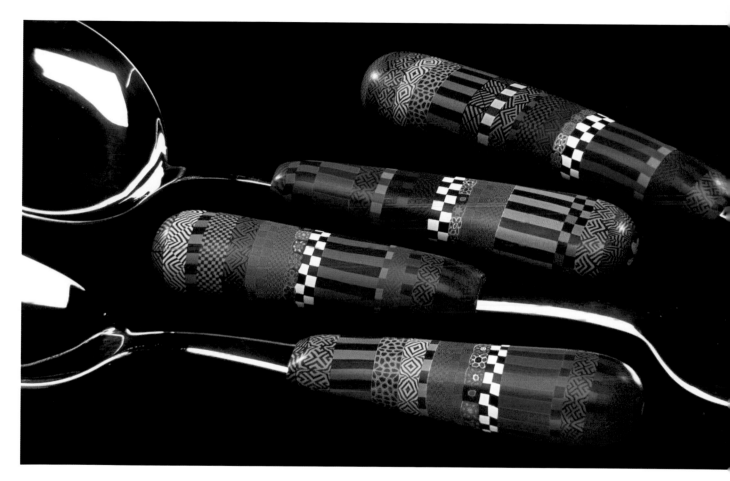

45

BARBARA BARRICK MCKIE

Precarious Balance, 2002
39 x 20 ¼ x ⅜" (99.1 x 51.4 x 1 cm)
Premo!; Delica beads, cotton; mokume gane, immersion
dying, machine appliqué, machine quilting
Photo by artist

MICHELLE ROSS

Renoir, 2002
3 ½ x 1 ¾ x 1 ½" (8.8 x 4.4 x 3.8 cm)
Kato Polyclay, Kato Clear Polyclay Medium; wood,
transferred image; stamped
Photo by Cassy Muronaka

CHRIS BIVINS

The Timekeeper, 2002
28 x 8 x 7" (71.1 x 20.3 x 17.5 cm)
Sculpey, Sculpey SuperFlex; copper
wire, fabric, wood
Photo by Gary Darby

Normally I make dolls that hang on
the wall, but I wanted something
more three-dimensional so I had the
idea of a seated figure. I discovered
that building a small twig chair isn't
as easy as I thought. *—CB*

LAYL MCDILL

Flying Story Lady, 2003
10 x 13 x 4" (25.4 x 33 x 10.2 cm)
Premo!; wire, glitter, transferred image; millefiori
Photo by artist

ELISE WINTERS

Bud Brooch, 2002
2 ¾ x 1 ½ x ½" (6.9 x 3.8 x 1.3 cm)
Fimo, Premo!; vermeil, crazed acrylic
Photo by Ralph Gabriner

RACHEL CARREN

Brooch, 2002
1 ½ x 2 ½ x ⅛" (3.8 x 6.3 x .3 cm)
Premo!; screened pattern, transferred image
Photo by Ralph Gabriner

This brooch is a color transfer of a
Japanese paper detail—done with gin as
the transfer agent! On top, a pattern of
dots and rods has been screened in gold
metallic paint. The contrast of a traditional
pattern with a contemporary one provides
depth and interest within the flat, two-
toned background. –RC

CATHERINE VERDIERE

Carnaval, 2003
14 ¼" (36 cm); pendant 3 ¼ x 1 ⅛"
 (8.5 x 3 cm)
Polymer clay; silver leaf, metal parts,
silver wire
Photo by Philippe Deneufve

GRANT DIFFENDAFFER

Blue Vase, 2003
12 x 3 ½ x 3 ½" (30.5 x 8.8 x 8.8 cm)
Premo!; glass; mokume gane, texturized
Photo by Kim Harrington

ROBERT WILEY

Coptic Ancient Book, 2002
3 x 3 x ½" (30.5 x 30.5 x 1.3 cm)
Premo!; paper; rubber stamped, rubbed, bound
with Coptic stitch
Photo by Rick Wells

KATHLEEN DUSTIN

Harem Woman Wallpiece, 1997
12 x 12 x 3" (30.5 x 30.5 x 7.5 cm)
Premo!; millefiori
Photo by George Post

The figure detaches and can be
connected to some pillow-shaped
beads to become a neckpiece. *–KD*

MARIE LAPRÉ GRABON

Fetish Doll with Book with Prayer to the Great Mother, 2003
14 x 8 x 2 ½" (35.6 x 20.3 x 6.3 cm)
Premo!; wire, feather, glass beads, applied gold leaf, papier-mâché
Photo by Jay Kennedy

MERRIE BUCHSBAUM

Polka Box, 2002
6 ½ x 2 ½ x 2 ½" (16.5 x 6.3 x 6.3 cm)
Fimo, Premo!; handbuilt, inlaid, stippled
Photo by John Polak

I love to make boxes. I'm particularly fond of
this one because it has such a feminine feel.
The polka dots dance and the box seems as
if at any moment it could wiggle and break
the stillness. –MB

MICHELLE ROSS

Ancient Rock Box, 2002
2 x 2 ½ x 1 ½" (5.1 x 6.3 x 3.8 cm)
Polymer clay; bamboo handle, brass charms,
acrylic paint, colored leaf; textured, rubber
stamped, antiqued
Photo by Cassy Muronaka

TERI BYRD

To Touch the Sun, 2001
26 ¼ x 4 ¾ x 4 ¾" (66.7 x 12.1 x 12.1 cm)
Premo!; paint; Skinner blend
Photo by Robert Batey

Teri Byrd's use of line and movement imparts
graceful animation to these skillfully sculpted
figures. *–ISD*

ROBERT WILEY

S.A.R. Egg, 2001
4 x 2 ¾ x 2 ¾" (10.2 x 7 x 7 cm)
Premo!; transferred image; rubber stamped
Photo by Rick Wells

With a background in math and engineering,
I wondered if it would be possible to make a
three-dimensional object by assembling flat
pieces of clay. –RW

ELISE WINTERS

Puff Bead Necklace, 1997
20" (50.8 cm)
Fimo, Premo!; vermeil, acrylic paint,
metallic leaf, PearlEx powders;
micromosaic, relief molded, stamped,
carved, woven
Photo by Ralph Gabriner

This necklace contains the first-ever
hollow beads formed over water-soluble
cornstarch packing peanuts. *–EW*

JEFFREY LLOYD DEVER

Cocoon–Double-Wall Seaform Vessel, 2002
11 ½ x 7 ½ x 7 ½" (29.2 x 19 x 19 cm)
Polymer clay
Photo by Gregory R. Staley

This piece is my first vessel experimenting with double-walled hollow form construction.
It was created for an invitational exhibit called Seeing Spots, curated by Steven Ford. *–JLD*

VALERIE MURCHAKE WRIGHT

Raku Vessel #1, 2003
9 x 6 ½" (22.9 x 16.5 cm)
Fimo, Kato Polyclay; PearlEx powders,
acrylic paint; textured
Photo by Kathy Shield

IRENE SEMANCHUK DEAN

3-Legged Vessel, 2003
5" (12.7 cm) x 2" (5 cm) diameter
Premo!; acrylic paint; hand formed, textured, painted
Photo by Stewart Stokes

APRIL ROSS

Tooth Fairy Rod Puppet, 2001
27 x 9 x 12" (68.6 x 22.9 x 30.5 cm)
Premo!, Sculpey III; copper wire, charms, coins, acrylic paint, fabric, lamb's
wool, wired ribbon, wood dowels, foil, construction wire
Photo by Jim Ross

The inspiration for my work was my life-long curiosity about the tooth fairy —
what does she look like, and what does she do with all those teeth? The part
that took the longest in her creation was making all those small teeth out of
polymer clay. But I feel the intricate teeth details, which make up the jewelry
and hair adornments, contribute to the fairy's authentic appearance. –AR

LAURA BALOMBINI

Two Fools, 2002
30 x 12 x 6" (76.2 x 30.5 x 15.2 cm)
Premo!; steel wire, steel mesh; molded
Photo by artist

Although the clay and wire work so
well together, the hard part is
sometimes engineering the piece to
stand or sit just right. *Two Fools* is
inspired by Cirque du Soleil. –LB

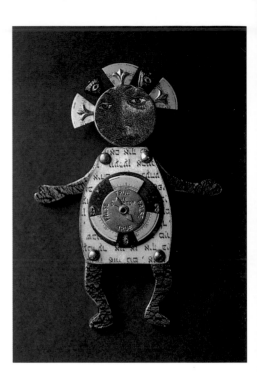

STEPHANIE JONES RUBIANO

True or False, 2002
¼ x 2 ½ x 3 ¾" (0.6 x 6.3 x 9.4 cm)
Premo!; gold leaf, vintage watch parts,
brass charms, transferred image
Photo by artist

KATHLEEN BOLAN

Haru Natsu (Spring Summer), 2003
1 ¼ x ⅞" (3.2 x 2.2 cm)
Fimo, Precious Metal Clay; 18k gold wire,
sterling silver, 22k gold leaf, photocopied
and transferred image; rubber stamped
Photo by Tim Thayer

SHARON MIHALYAK

Remember..., 2001
10 x 10 x 1" (25.4 x 25.4 x 2.5 cm)
Sculpey; wood picture frame, oil paint; printed,
relief etched, textured, antiqued
Photo by Chuck May

I was moved to create this after 9/11. –SM

LUANN UDELL

Riverstone Necklace, 2001
24" (61 cm)
Polymer clay
Photo by Jeff Baird

My entire body of work—jewelry, mixed-media
wall hangings, and sculptures—is inspired by
the prehistoric art of the Lascaux cave in
France. I use faux ivory made from polymer
clay to make artifacts such as tiny horses, fish,
bones, beads, buttons, shells, and stones.
Using modern materials, I create artifacts of a
lost culture, an imagined prehistory. *—LU*

MARCIA PETERSON

The Princess, 2003
9 x 6 x 5" (22.9 x 15.2 x 12.7 cm)
Sculpey SuperFlex, ProMat; wire, silk,
silk velvet, wool
Photo by Lynn Thompson

JEANETTE KANDRAY

Fractured Rainbow, 2003
8 x 4 x 4" (20.3 x 10.2 x 10.3 cm)
Kato Polyclay; pearlescent inks, glass vase
Photo by Karen Carter

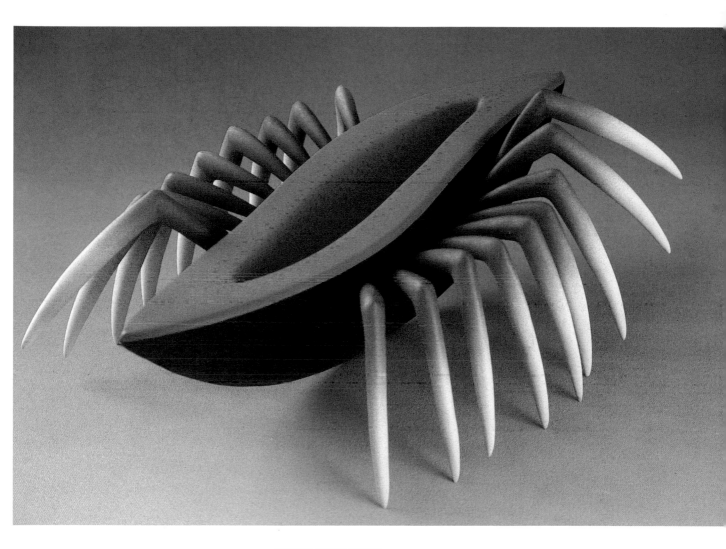

JEFFREY LLOYD DEVER

Crawl–Double-Wall Vessel with Movable Legs, 2003
4 ½ x 10 ½ x 17 ¼" (11.4 x 27.9 x 42.8 cm)
Polymer clay; wire
Photo by Gregory R. Staley

Crawl was born out of the notion of locomotion. For an exhibit with the theme
of movement, I explored many ideas in sketches and several attempts at
engineering various leg forms. *–JLD*

MARIE LAPRÉ GRABON

Fetish Doll With Birds, 2003
14 x 5 x 2 ½" (35.6 x 12.7 x 6.3 cm)
Premo!; wire, glass beads, wood
Photo by Jay Kennedy

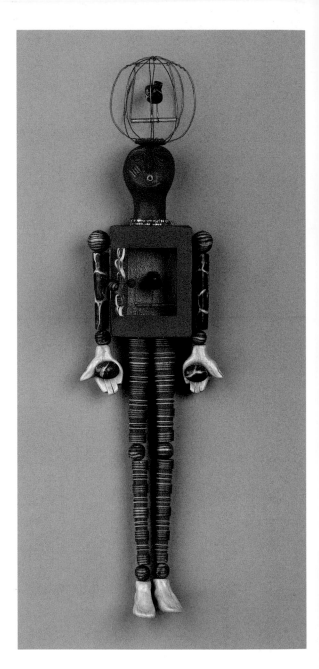

CYNTHIA TOOPS
CHUCK DOMITROVICH

Night Moves, 2002
2 x 2 ½ x 2 ¼" (5.1 x 6.3 x 5.7 cm)
Fimo, Sculpey III; sterling silver, garnet; micromosaic threads
Jewelry by Chuck Domitrovich
Photo by Roger Schreiber

This bracelet takes its cue from old Moroccan enameled bracelets. *–CT*

BONNIE MERCHANT

Picnic, 2002
19 x 7" (47.5 x 17.5 cm)
Fimo, Premo!; electric socket and bulb
Photo by Jason Kinch

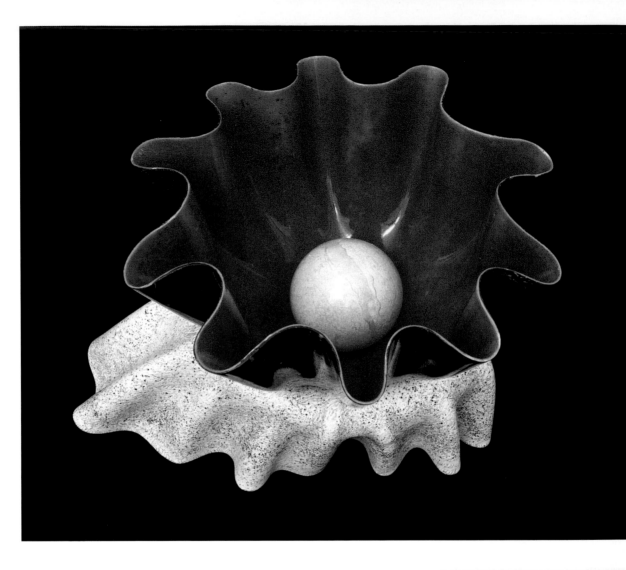

JAMES LEHMAN

Mother Of Pearl, 2002
9 x 14 x 10" (22.9 x 10.2 x 25.4 cm)
Premo!, Sculpey III; finished with water-based
polyurethane hardwood floor finish
Photo by artist

CHRISTINE DICKERSON

Autumnal Spirit Pin, 2002
4 ½ x 2 ½ x ½" (11.4 x 6.3 x 1.3 cm)
Premo!; feathers, beads
Photo by Karen Carter

CYNTHIA TOOPS
DAN ADAMS

Guardian of the Small House, 2001
3 x 2 x ¾" (7.5 x 5.1 x 1.9 cm)
Polymer clay; rice, seeds
Glass elements by Dan Adams
Photo by Roger Schreiber

IRENE YURKEWYCH

Amber Mosaic Box, 2001
8 x 5 x 7" (20.3 x 12.7 x 17.5 cm)
Premo!; mosaic application
Photo by Howard Marr

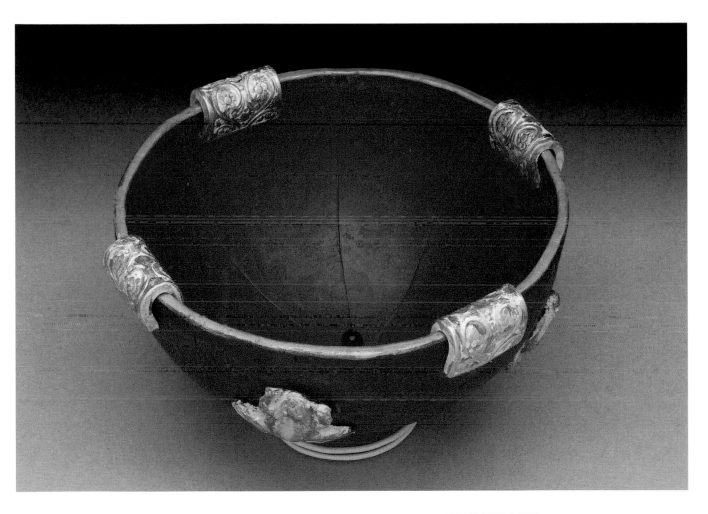

LOUISE FISCHER COZZI

Ceremonial Frog Bowl 2, 2002
2 $\frac{5}{8}$ x 4 $\frac{7}{8}$ x $\frac{1}{8}$" (6.5 x 12.5 x .3 cm)
Premo!, Fimo, Liquid Sculpey; acrylic paint, ink, pencil;
molded, extruded
Photo by George Post

CAROLYN POTTER

Creation, 2002
18 x 18 x 9" (45.7 x 45.7 x 22.9 cm)
Premo!; gourd, acrylic paint; mosaic, Skinner
blend, inlay
Photo by Corie Photography

The harmonious use of line, shape, and
negative space unify the surface design with
the object in this handsomely decorated gourd
by Carolyn Potter. *–ISD*

BANKS!

Nono Nono, 1998
8 x 6 x 8" (20.3 x 15.2 x 20.3 cm)
Premo!; wire mesh
Photo by Hap Sakwa

DEBBIE KRUEGER

Aquarium Vase, 1997
4 ¾ x 6 x 3 ½" (12.1 x 15.2 x 8.8 cm)
Fimo; silver leaf, glitter; canework inlay, mokume gane,
sculptural relief, inlay, sanded, buffed
Photo by George Post

Using a translucent layering technique I learned from
Kathleen Dustin, I was able to create the illusion of
depth in this piece. *–DK*

JEFFREY LLOYD DEVER

Stickpins–Nature Form Trio, 2003
Longest 7" (17.5 cm)
Polymer clay; silver pins
Photo by Gregory R. Staley

CYNTHIA BELJAN

Tribal Warrior, 2002
3 ¼ x 2 ¼ x ¾" (8.3 x 5.7 x 1.9 cm)
Premo!; rubber cord, copper wire,
brass beads; inlaid
Photo by Amy Widerman

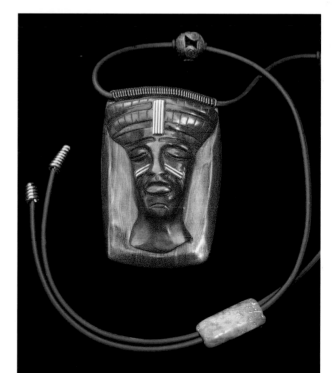

CATHERINE VERDIERE

Colliers "Art Optique," 2003
14 ¼" (36 cm); rectangular pendant
2 ½ x 1" (6.5 x 2.5 cm); teardrop
pendant 2 ½ x 2" (6.5 x 5 cm)
Polymer clay; metal parts, silver wire
Photo by Philippe Deneufve

These two pieces were inspired by
the fabulous work of the painter
Victor Vassarely. –CV

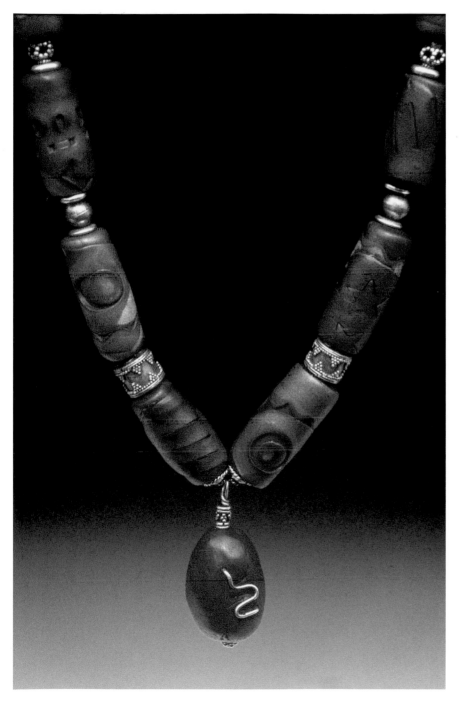

SYBILLE HAMILTON

Untitled, 2003
Polymer clay; Bali silver beads
Photo by Laura Timmins

JODY BISHEL

Dios, 1999
8 x 6 x 6" (20.3 x 15.2 x 15.2 cm)
Premo!, Liquid Sculpey, Translucent Liquid
Sculpey; oil paint, sea glass
Photo by Daniel Buckley

DAYLE DOROSHOW

Messenger From Pompeii, 2002
7 x 7 x 2" (17.5 x 17.5 x 5.1 cm)
Fimo; silver, wood, transferred photographic emulsion
Photo by Don Felton

This new work explores the meeting of polymer clay and photography and allows photographs to become sculptural as they float outside, inside, and around pieces of clay. –DD

ELIZABETH LANDT

Archer King, 2003
13 ½ x 5 ½ x 5" (34.3 x 14 x 12.7 cm)
Sculpey, Sculpey SuperFlex; acrylic paint,
arrow tips, found metal, washers, copper
wire, turquoise beads, glass beads, sheepskin
Photo by Daniel Landt

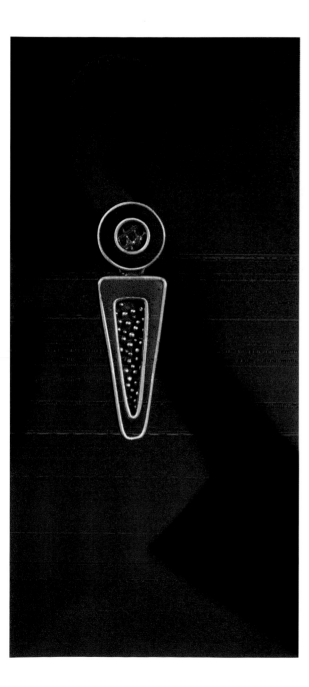

JUDY KUSKIN

Untitled (Earring), 2003
2 ½ x ¾ x ¼" (6.3 x 1.9 x .6 cm)
Premo!, Fimo, Precious Metal Clay; fine
silver wire
Photo by Penina Meisels

JEANETTE KANDRAY

Amber Necklace, 2002
1 x 24 x 1" (2.5 x 61 x 2.5 cm)
Premo!; glass and wooden beads, imitation leather cord
Photo by Karen Carter

GERRI NEWFRY

Eastern Elements Collage Frames, 2002
Larger: 3 x 4 x ½" (7.5 x 10.2 x 1.3 cm)
Premo!, Translucent Liquid Sculpey; paper,
acrylic, silver composite leaf, transferred image,
decorative foil, chalk, acrylic wash; millefiori,
rubber stamped, decoupage
Photo by Larry Sanders

IRWIN WALKENFELD

Funerary Urn #1, 2002
8 x 4 x 4" (20.3 x 10.2 x 10.2 cm)
Premo!, Sculpey III; artistic wire, eyelets
Photo by artist

Like most of my work, the funerary urn
has features that elicit interaction: a
door that opens, an opening that can
be reversed, a jigsaw puzzle with
movable pieces. −*IW*

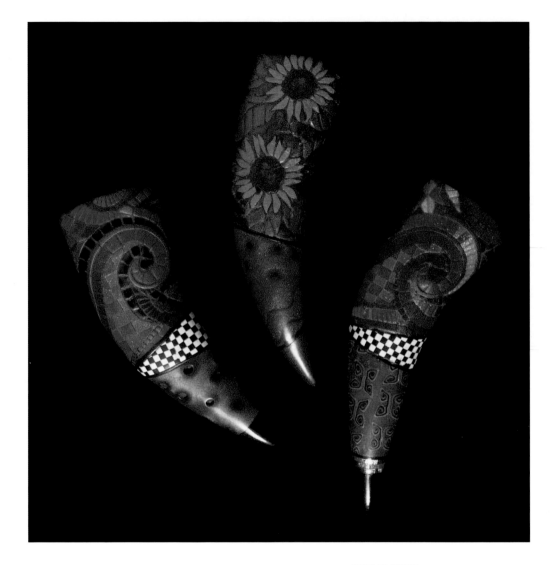

AMELIA HELM

Sabre Brooches, 2000
3 x ¾ x ½" (7.5 x 1.9 x 1.3 cm)
Polymer clay

JILL ACKIRON-MOSES

Fall Necklace, 2000
18" (45.7 cm)
Premo!; telephone wire, gold leaf
Photo by Hap Sakwa

ANGIE WIGGINS

Platters–Group Shot, 2002
7 x 2 ½ x 6 ½" (17.5 x 6.3 x 16.5 cm)
Fimo; Skinner blend, laminated, canework,
surface texture
Photo by Taylor Dabney

SHANE SMITH

Don't It Make Your Red Rooster Blue?, 2002
11 x 10 x 5" (27.9 x 25.4 x 12.7 cm)
Premo!; ceramic armature; canework
Photo by Jennifer Hanson

A blues-music radio program called "The
Red Rooster Lounge" inspired this piece.

—SS

ELISE WINTERS

Flair Stickpin, 2002
4 ½ x 3 x ½" (11.3 x 7.5 x 1.3 cm)
Fimo, Premo!; mica, crazed acrylic
Photo by Ralph Gabriner

BARBARA SPERLING

Hummingbird Pendant, 2002
3 ¾ x 2" (9.4 x 5.1 cm)
Fimo, Sculpey III, Precious Metal Clay; metallic leaf, metallic rub,
sterling silver chain; millefiori canework, mokume gane, impression
molded, textured and formed, antiqued
Photo by Robert Diamante

Combining the polymer with PMC is a challenge. I make the two work
cohesively, without the PMC overtaking my millefiori work, by carrying
the polymer theme into the PMC. –BS

LAURA TIMMINS

Bracelet, 2003
2 x 4 x 4" (5.1 x 10.2 x 10.2 cm)
Premo!; silver beads
Photo by artist

KLEW [KAREN LEWIS]

Untitled, 2000
24" (61 cm)
Polymer clay; vintage glass, metal findings

LYNNE ANN SCHWARZENBERG

Tibetan Prayer Beads Wearable Windchime, 2002
36" (91.4 cm); pendant 4 x ¾ x ¾"
 (10.2 x 1.9 x 1.9 cm)
Premo!; glass and metal beads, brass chimes, PearlEx
powder, paint
Photo by Harold Shapiro

LAURIE MIKA

Dia de los Muertos (Day of the Dead), 2002
12 x 9 x 1" (30.5 x 22.9 x 2.5 cm)
Sculpey, Premo!; PearlEx powders, micro mosaics, jewelry, milagros, broken china, paint
Photo by artist

This icon celebrates the Mexican holiday honoring the dead. I wanted it to be an altar-like piece using milagros that I have collected. There's a little bit of everything in this piece, but I feel that it's well integrated. –LM

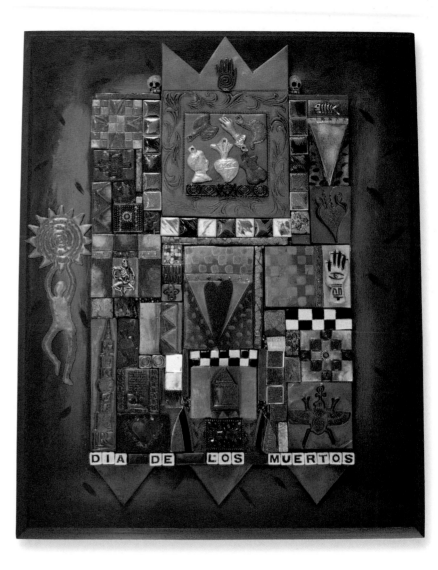

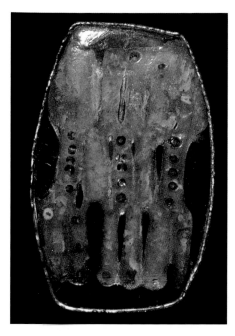

MARGARET KRISTOF

Mysterium Series, 2002
1 ¾ x 1 ¾" (4.4 x 4.4 cm)
Polymer clay; seed beads, origami
paper, paint, brass bezel
Photo by Pad McLauglin

NAN ROCHE

3 Nodawa Collars, 2002
4 x 7 x ¼" (10.2 x 17.5 x .6 cm)
Polymer clay; rubber cording; press
molded, riveted, patinaed
Photo by artist

The *nodawa* was a chin and neck
guard in the armor of the Japanese
samurai. −NR

Nan Roche's highly tactile work
expresses strong cultural
influences, with a vibrant interaction
between organic imagery and the
design's geometry. −ISD

BARBARA SPERLING

Harmony, 2000
8 x 6 x 1" (20.3 x 15.2 x 2.5 cm)
Fimo; gold leaf, gold wire, pendant adapter,
transferred image; millefiori canework,
mokume gane, faux stone effects, etched,
stamped with leather tools
Photo by Robert Diamante

Barbara Sperling has blended several
techniques in this intricate mixed-media
piece, which radiates tranquility with its
soothing colors, forms, and symmetry. *–ISD*

KRISTA WELLS

Domed-Top Box, 2000
3 ½ x 6 ¾ x 3 ½" (8.8 x 17.1 x 8.8 cm)
Premo!; wire; textured
Photo by Julian Beveridge

With this piece, rather than imitate wood or metal, I'm
taking advantage of polymer clay's intrinsic strengths: the
ability to hold texture, form, and luster. –KW

KATHLEEN DUSTIN

Kneeling Village Woman–Purse, 1999
6 x 5 x 4" (15.2 x 12.7 x 10.2 cm)
Premo!, Sculpey III, liquid polymer; colored
pencil, gold leaf; layered, sanded, polished
Photo by George Post

MERRIE BUCHSBA

3 Part Necklace, 2(
1 ¾ x 6 x ⅝" (4.4
Fimo; ground herbs
Photo by John Polak

I love cooking, so
incorporating them
seems natural to m

KLEW [KAREN LEWIS]

Mardi Gras, 2001
10 x 8 x 3" (25.4 x 20.3 x 7.5 cm)
Polymer clay; glass beads; canework
Photo by artist

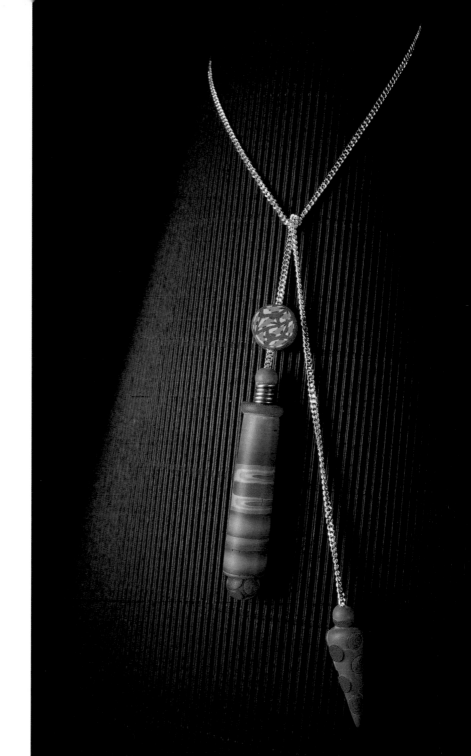

CATHERINE VERDIERE

Reflects, 2003
17 ¾" (45 cm); larger pendant 3 ¼ x 5 ¼"
  (8.5 x 13.5 cm)
Polymer clay; wire, silver chain
Photo by Philippe Deneufve

JULIA CONVERSE SOBER

Fragments Under Glass, 2002
3 x 1 x ¼" (7.5 x 2.5 x .6 cm)
Translucent Liquid Sculpey; colored pencil, silver leaf, microscope slides, metal
tubing, wire, metal tape; pencil transfer
Photo by Larry Sanders

While experimenting with colored-pencil transfers to create larger pieces, I
realized that the edge trimmings and partially successful transfer bits had an
appeal all their own. Collaging these pieces together gave the fragments, which
I'd previously considered waste, a whole new life! *–JCS*

VICTORIA L. GRIMES

Necklace of Leaves, 2002
Longest 23 x 1 ½ x 1 ½" (58.4 x 3.8 x 3.8 cm)
Premo!; beads, embossing powders, telephone
wire, adhesive, bead wire, sterling silver clasp;
Skinner blend
Photo by Jerry Anthony

KATHERINE DEWEY

Follow, 2001
5 x 3 x 4" (12.7 x 7.5 x 10.2 cm)
Premo!; brass wire and glue-sized paper
armature, sisal fiber, acetate, acrylic paint,
water-based oil paint; dyed, hand embossed
Photo by James Clay Walls

ERICA SHAVER

Untitled, 1999
6 x 5 x 5" (15.2 x 12.7 x 12.7 cm)
Fimo; sterling silver, freshwater pearls
Photo by Sharon Massey

Erica Shaver uses the irregular surfaces of hammered silver and freshwater
pearls, plus the "placqueing" on the polymer clay, to create a subtle marriage of
complementary textures on this vessel-like object. –*ISD*

MARISOL ROSS

Rhythm, 2002
24 x 12 x 2 ½" (61 x 30.5 x 6.3 cm)
Sculpey, Premo!; mosaic grout, dirt, acrylic
paint, plywood
Photo by Peter Jacobs

Marisol Ross uses a multimedia approach
to create a rich three-dimensional and
painterly effect. Exciting textures and
vigorous line quality animate this narrative
scene. *−ISD*

LYDIA MARR

Horse Head Relief, 2003
9 x 10 ½ x 1 ½" (22.9 x 26.7 x 3.8 cm)
Fimo; patina
Photo by artist

LAURA TABAKMAN

I'm Not Ready, 2002
17 ½ x 6 ½ x 4 ½" (44.5 x 16.5 x 11.4 cm)
Premo!; aluminum wire, oil paint
Photo by artist

DEBRA DE WOLFF

Collection of Bracelets, 2003
Largest 2 ½ x 1" (6.3 x 2.5 cm)
Polymer clay; memory wire
Photo by Maria Ellen Huebner

GWEN GIBSON

Mad Caps, 2002
18" (45.7 cm); beads 1" (2.5 cm)
Premo!; silver bead caps, paint; textured
Photo by Robert Diamante

ANNIE M.

Firewalker, 1999
2 ¾ x 2 ¼ x ⅜" (7 x 5.7 x .9 cm)
Fimo
Photo by Jerry Anthony

MAJ-BRITT CAWTHON

Freeform #5, 2002
3 ½" (8.8 cm)
Fimo; silver tube, silver snake chain with
friction clasp; canework
Photo by John Bonath, Maddog Studios

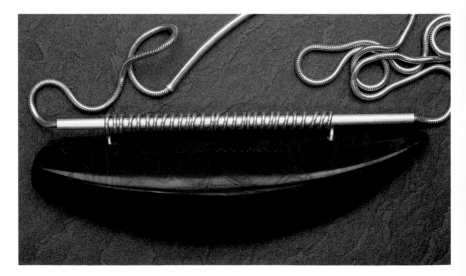

WENDY WALLIN MALINOW

Blue Triangles, 2001
22" (55.9 cm)
Liquid polymer clay; rubber, transferred image
Photo by Courtney Frisse

LUANN UDELL

Mammoth Ivory Neckpiece, 2001
24" (61 cm)
Polymer clay
Photo by Jeff Baird

ELISE WINTERS

Shell Necklace, 2001
18" (45.7 cm)
Fimo, Premo!; vermeil, crazed acrylic
Photo by Ralph Gabriner

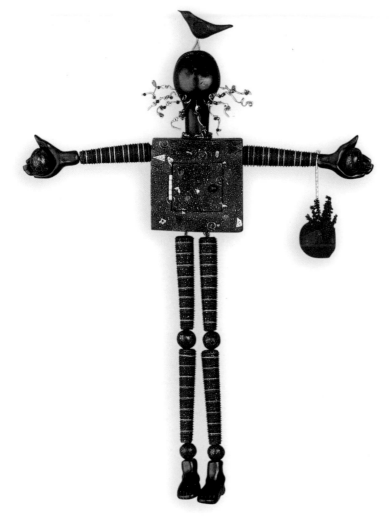

MARIE LAPRÉ GRABON

Fetish Doll With Helping Spirit, 2003
14 x 8 x 2" (35.6 x 20.3 x 5.1 cm)
Premo!; wire, glass beads, pipe cleaner,
gold leaf, papier-mâché
Photo by Jay Kennedy

BARBARA MORRISON

Mitochondrial DNA: The Totem Pole, 2002
24 x 4 x 3" (61 x 10.2 x 7.5 cm)
Fimo, Sculpey; wood
Photo by Patrick Clark

KATHLEEN DUSTIN

Polished Face Beads–Neckpiece, 1999
18" (45.7 cm); largest bead 3 ½" (5.1 to 8.8 cm)
Premo!, Sculpey III, liquid polymer; colored pencil, gold leaf;
layered, sanded, polished
Photo by George Post

GERRI NEWFRY

Zen Sunset Journal, 2002
5 ¾ x 4 ½ x 1" (14.6 x 11.4 x 2.5 cm)
Premo!; silver leaf, waxed linen,
archival papers, acrylic; millefiori,
Skinner blend, rubber stamped
Photo by Larry Sanders

I've been fascinated with books all
my life, and with polymer clay for
the last decade. Putting the two
together was only natural. I create
the covers entirely from clay, and
hand-bind the archival text block
using either an ancient Coptic
method or accordion pleating. *–GN*

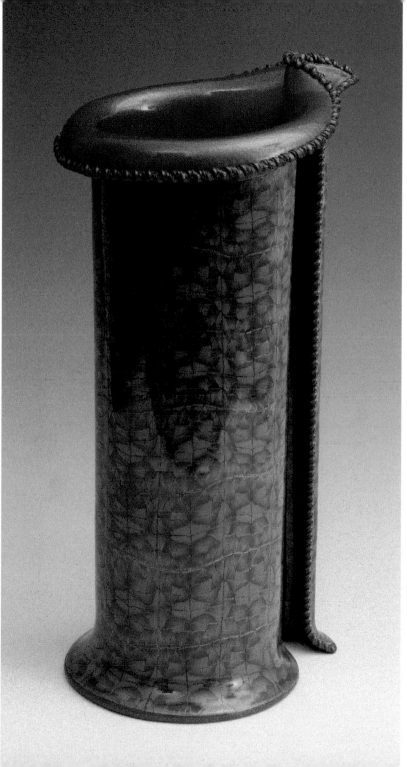

LAURA TIMMINS

Vessel, 2002
13 x 5 x 6" (33 x 12.7 x 15.2 cm)
Polymer clay; wire mesh armature
Photo by artist

JEAN COHEN

Fiesta, 2003
2 ¾ x 4 ¾ x 3 ½" (7 x 12.1 x 8.8 cm)
Polymer clay; sterling bead, metal hinge, reverse transferred image; Skinner blend, inlaid
Photo by Norman Watkins

SHANE SMITH

Wish You Were Here, 2000
14 x 7 x 7" (35.6 x 17.5 x 17.5 cm)
Premo!, Sculpey; wood, telephone wire,
glass beads, cubic zirconia
Photo by Jennifer Hanson

KAREN WOODS

Marriage, 2002
5 x 4 x 5" (12.7 x 10.2 x 12.7 cm)
Polymer clay; reed basket, natural vine, glass beads;
hand-dyed, netted weaving

KATHLEEN DUSTIN

Face With Screen Purse, 2000
4 x 4 x 2" (10.2 x 10.2 x 5.1 cm)
Liquid polymer; steel, transferred image
Photo by George Post

ANNABELLE FISHER

Rainbow Bug Beads, 2002
1 x ⁷⁄₈ x ³⁄₈" (2.5 x 2.2 x .9 cm)
Fimo; millefiori
Photo by Jerry Anthony

KLEW [KAREN LEWIS]

Untitled, 2002
3 x ¹⁄₂ x 2 ¹⁄₂" (7.5 x 1.3 x 6.3 cm)
Polymer clay; canework

Karen Lewis used caneworking, hand forming,
and imitative techniques to create a piece with
the look of an ancient carved relief. —ISD

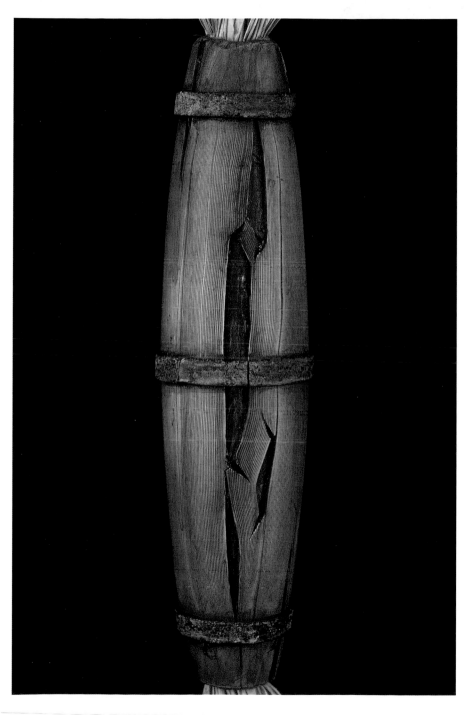

DIANE W. VILLANO

Big Bead–Fossilized Wood, 2001
6 x 1 ¼ x 1 ¼" (15.8 x 3.2 x 3.2 cm)
Premo!; wood, acrylic paint
Photo by William K. Sacco

LOUISE FISCHER COZZI

Sa-Sa Necklace, 2002
1 ½ x 16 ½ x 3 ³⁄₃₂" (1.3 x 41.9 x 7.7 cm)
Premo!, Fimo; telephone wire, paint, brass findings,
antique glass beads; etched, carved
Photo by George Post

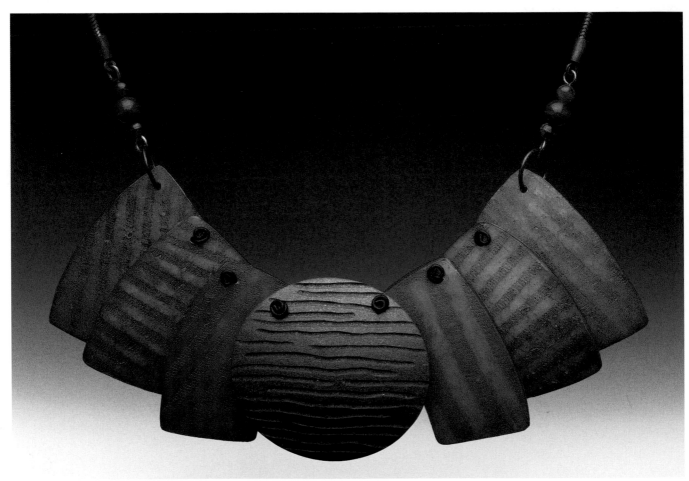

PAT PETTYJOHN

Night Watch, 2003
3 ½ x 1 ¾ x ¾" (8.8 x 4.4 x 1.9 cm)
Fimo; patina, Buna cord
Photo by John Lucas

SANDRA MCCAW

Untitled, 2001
2 ½ x 1 ¼ x ⅛" (6.3 x 3.2 x .3 cm)
Fimo; 23k gold leaf
Photo by Jeff Baird

The cord on this piece contains
over 800 polymer beads to create a
shaded effect. It was a very short-
lived phase! *–SM*

ELIZABETH LANDT

Bolt Queen, 1999
14 x 8 x 3" (35.6 x 20.3 x 7.5 cm)
Sculpey; acrylic paint, found objects
Photo by Daniel Landt

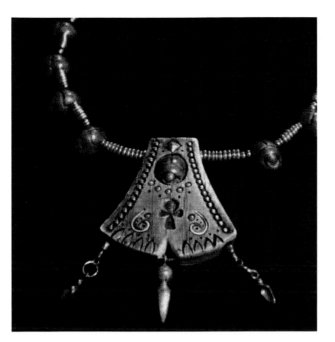

JOHNNY KUBORSSY

Nefertiti, 2003
17" (43.2 cm); pendant 2 ¼ x 2 x ¼" (5.7 x 5.1 x .6 cm)
Premo!; brass findings, nickel wire, brass and copper drop beads, jewelry wire, acrylic paint; molded, rubber stamped, etched
Photo by Jim Ciarico

NAN ROCHE

Celtic Collar, 2002
3 ½ x 7 x ½" (8.8 x 17.5 x 1.3 cm)
Premo!; rubber cording; extruded, layered, braided
Photo by artist

OLIVIA ASH TURNER

Ashes to Ashes..., 2002
15 ½ x 10 x 3" (39.4 x 25.4 x 7.5 cm)
Premo!; gold leaf, PearlEx powders
Photo by artist

Leaves are a recurring motif in my work. I
envisioned *Ashes to Ashes...* during a dark
chapter in my battle with cancer. During the
therapeutic creation period I found peace.

—OAT

ELIZABETH LANDT

Siren, 2003
20 x 9 x 1" (50.8 x 22.9 x 2.5 cm)
Sculpey, Sculpey SuperFlex; PearlEx powders, copper
wire, beads, glitter, gold leaf, gold rub, acrylic paint,
photocopied transferred image; rubber stamped
Photo by Daniel Landt

JULIA CONVERSE SOBER

Cellular Pendant and Earrings, 2002
Pendant 2 x 1 ½ x ¾" (5.8 x 3.8 x 1.9 cm);
earrings 2 x 1 ½ x ¼" (5.1 x 3.8 x .6 cm)
Premo!; metal tubing, hardware, wire
Photo by Larry Sanders

The resemblance of these simple canes to complex
cellular structures appeals to my inner scientist. –*JCS*

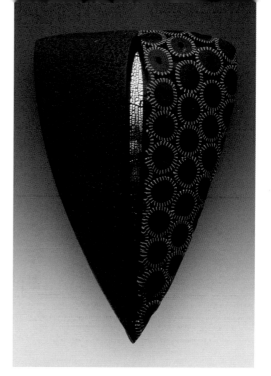

MARGARET REGAN

Black Texture Brooch, 2002
2 ½ x 1 ½ x ½" (6.3 x 3.8 x 1.3 cm)
Polymer clay; silver leaf
Photo by George Post

Margaret Regan created an exciting dimensional
effect in this piece. Black and white canework
balances its intense texture and coloration, yet the
two surface treatments are neatly unified by a
single brilliant flash of silver. –*ISD*

OLIVE ALPERT

Chrysler Building Pin, 1998
4 ½ x 1 ¼ x ⅛" (11.4 x 3.2 x .3 cm)
Cernit, Fimo, Sculpey
Photo by artist

AMELIA HELM

Mosaic Mat, 1995
30 x 26 x 1 ½" (76.2 x 66.1 x 3.8 cm)
Polymer clay
Photo by Debra Rueb

MARGARET REGAN

Sheen Bangle Bracelets, 2002
3 x 3 ¼ x ½" (7.5 x 8.3 x 1.3 cm)
Polymer clay; elastic
Photo by Robert K. Liu/Ornament

Clean and precise, these bracelets exude a quiet elegance
with sophisticated colors and satiny finishes. −ISD

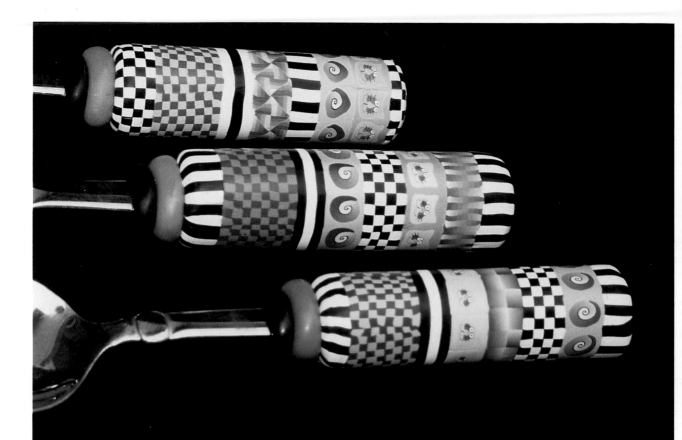

KAREN SCUDDER

Untitled, 2002
2 x 9 x 1" (5.1 x 22.9 x 2.5 cm)
Premo!; stainless steel utensils
Photo by artist

MONA KISSEL

Asian Cherry Blossom Reversible Necklace, 2002
20 x 5 x ½" (50.8 x 12.7 x 1.3 cm)
Kato Polyclay; gold leaf, PearlEx powders, ink; rubber stamped
Photo by artist

VICTORIA L. GRIMES

Geranium Basket Purse, 2001
10 ½ x 9 x 6 ½" (26.7 x 22.9 x 16.5 cm)
Premo!; vintage wooden purse, telephone wire, contact cement, adhesive, satin varnish; formed, molded, extruded
Photo by Jerry Anthony

I'm a gardener, but while recovering from surgery, I missed some of my favorite spring projects, so instead I was inspired to decorate a vintage purse with polymer clay. *–VLG*

IRWIN WALKENFELD

Bloxes–Tower with Windows, 2002
12 x 7 x 5" (30.5 x 17.5 x 12.7 cm)
Premo!, Sculpey III
Photo by artist

This is just one structure/sculpture
that can be constructed from my set of
stackable and linkable boxes. What I
especially like is that you never know
what to expect. Each box is unique so
it's always a surprise what the final
construction will look like. *–IW*

NANCY MOSELEY
LISA WIDELL

Graduation Day, 2003
3 ½ x 3 ¾ x ½" (8.8 x 9.4 x 1.3 cm)
Fimo; canework
Photo by Rob Ratkowski

141

SANDRA MCCAW

Untitled, 2002
1 ½ x ½ x ¹⁄₁₆" (3.8 x 1.3 x .2 cm)
Polymer clay; 23k gold leaf
Photo by Jeff Baird

DIANE W. VILLANO

Big Bead–Turquoise in Braided Silver, 2002
5 x 5 x 2 ¼" (12.7 x 12.7 x 5.7 cm)
Premo!; wood, mica powder, kumihimo cord
Photo by William K. Sacco

JULIA CONVERSE SOBER

Cellular Specimen Set, 2003
Pendant 3 x 1 x ¼" (7.5 x 2.5 x .6 cm); earrings: 2 x ¾ x ¼" (5.1 x 1.9 x .6 cm)
Premo!; microscope slides, metal tubing, gold-filled wire, sterling silver, glass beads; canework
Photo by Larry Sanders

An obsession to combine microscope slides with caned patterns led to these pieces. The clarity of glass slides allows for embellishment on either side of a piece, the hinged construction of the earrings allows for a flip-over change from one look to another, and the cell-like appearance of compound bull's-eye canes makes for a natural pairing with these tools of science. *–JCS*

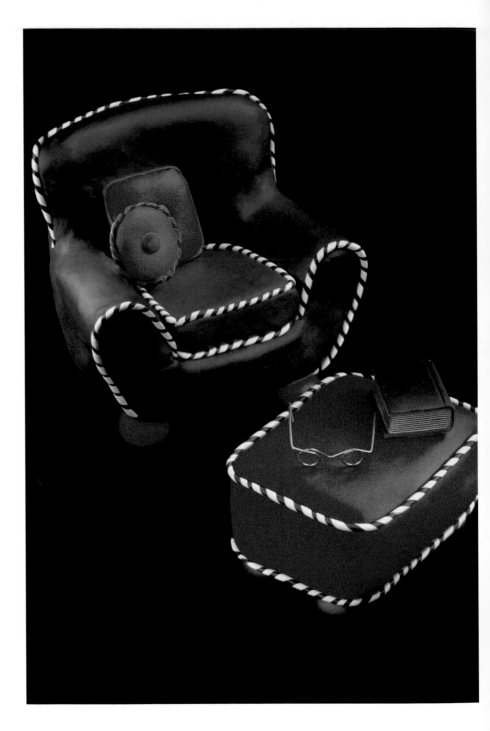

VIRGINIA V. SPERRY

Purple Chair with Yellow Ottoman, 1999
3 x 3 x 6" (7.5 x 7.5 x 15.2 cm)
Premo!; tin foil armature
Photo by Herrmann/Starke

I was a theater major in college, and have
entire set designs in my head. My furniture
creations are a small component of that.
—VVS

KATHLEEN DUSTIN

Saint #5–Evening Purse, 2003
7 x 4 x 3" (17.5 x 10.2 x 7.5 cm)
Premo!, Sculpey III, liquid polymer;
colored pencil, gold leaf, Viton rubber
handle; layered, sanded, polished
Photo by George Post

VICKI RHINE

Starcatcher, 1992
8 x 4 x ½" (20.3 x 10.2 x 1.3 cm)
Premo!; wire, twigs, waxed linen, PearlEx
powders; Skinner blend, millefiori
Photo by Randy Ada

JUDY SUMMER

Black Stallion, 2003
15 x 8 x 4" (38.1 x 20.3 x 10.2 cm)
Premo!; wire armature with copper tubing and foil,
pins; stamped, textured
Photo by Debra Dietz

MARGARET KRISTOF

The Girls, 2001
Largest 6 ½ x 1 ½ x ½" (16.5 x 3.8 x 1.3 cm)
Polymer clay; seed beads, wood dowel, acrylic paint
Photo by Pad McLaughlin

JOHN EDDINGTON

Bull Elk, 2001
8 x 4 x 9" (20.3 x 10.2 x 22.9 cm)
Polymer clay; stainless steel, acrylic paint
Photo by artist

OLIVE ALPERT

Mermaid Pendant, 1998
3 ⁵⁄₈ x 3 ¹⁄₈ x ⁵⁄₁₆" (9.1 x 8.3 x .8 cm)
Fimo; acrylic paint
Photo by artist

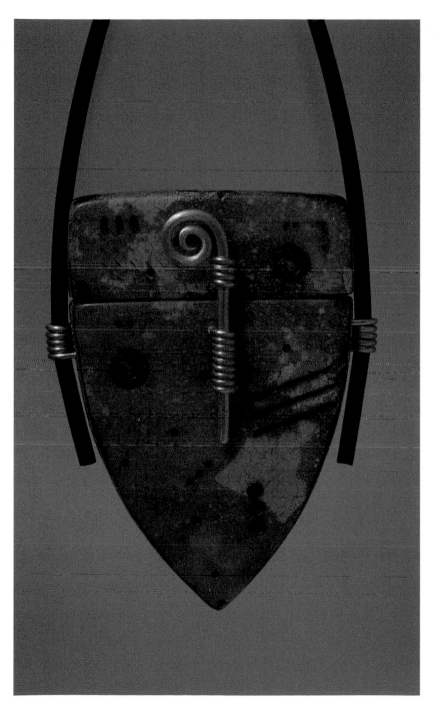

LAURA TABAKMAN

Locket, 2002
2 ½ x 1 ⅝ x ¾" (6.3 x 4.1 x 1.9 cm)
Premo!; wire lock, Buna cord holders, hinges, metallic foils, acrylic paint; stamped, sanded, polished
Photo by artist

WENDY WALLIN MALINOW

Gossip, 2001
6 x 6 x 12" (15.2 x 15.2 x 30.5 cm)
Polymer clay; transferred image, paper
Photo by Courtney Frisse

RACHEL GOURLEY

Spondylosis, 2003
14 ½" (36.8 cm)
Fimo, Premo!; sand
Photo by Nan Roche

Each of these intriguing pieces is an
incredible tactile experience in itself; together
they present a visual feast of spikes, cracks,
amoeba-like dots, grains, piercing, glassy
smoothness, and more. –ISD

GWEN GIBSON

Frosted Bead Necklace, 2003
21" (53.3 cm) long
Premo!, translucent polymer clay; silver findings, silkscreen
Photo by Robert Diamante

DESIREE McCROREY

Golden-Toned Ellipsoidal Beads, 2001
1 ¼ x ¾ x ¾" (3.2 x 1.9 x 1.9 cm)
Polymer clay
Photo by Liv Ames

SANDRA MCCAW

Untitled, 2002
1 ¼ x 2 ¼ x ⅛" (3.2 x 5.7 x .3 cm)
Fimo; 23k gold leaf
Photo by Jeff Baird

Sandra McCaw is known for her dimensional, symmetrical canework. Note her subtle use of asymmetry with several small gold-leaf accents. *–ISD*

BARBARA SPERLING

White Waterlily Brooch, 2001
2 ½ x 1 ¾" (6.3 x 4.4 cm)
Fimo; gold and metallic leaf, metallic rub, gold
wire, freshwater pearl; millefiori canework,
textured, molded
Photo by Robert Diamante

JACQUELINE LEE

The Pharaoh, 2000
2 x 1 ½ x ¼" (5.1 x 3.8 x .6 cm)
Premo!; acrylic paints
Photo by Sherri Haab

155

LILIAN CANOUET

Dragonfly Jar, 2001
5 ¾ x 3 ½ x 3 ½" (14.6 x 8.8 x 8.8 cm)
Premo!, Sculpey; glass jar

KLEW [KAREN LEWIS]

Untitled, 2002
2 x 1 x 1" (5.1 x 2.5 x 2.5 cm)
Polymer clay; canework
Photo by Marcia Albert

CAROLYN POTTER

Virgin, 2003
7 x 5 x 1 ½" (17.5 x 12.7 x 3.8 cm)
Fimo, Sculpey SuperFlex; aluminum foil
armature; mokume gane
Photo by Corie Photography

LYNNE ANN SCHWARZENBERG

The Best of Friends, 2002
5 ½ x 5 ½ x 5" (14 x 14 x 12.7 cm)
Premo!, Sculpey Granitex; acrylic paint
Photo by Harold Shapiro

For my dad's 65th birthday I wanted to capture the special
relationship between him and his dog, Hobo. –*LAS*

WENDY WALLIN MALINOW

Face Bracelet, 2002
3 ½ x 3 x 2" (8.8 x 7.5 x 5.1 cm)
Polymer clay; inlay
Photo by Courtney Frisse

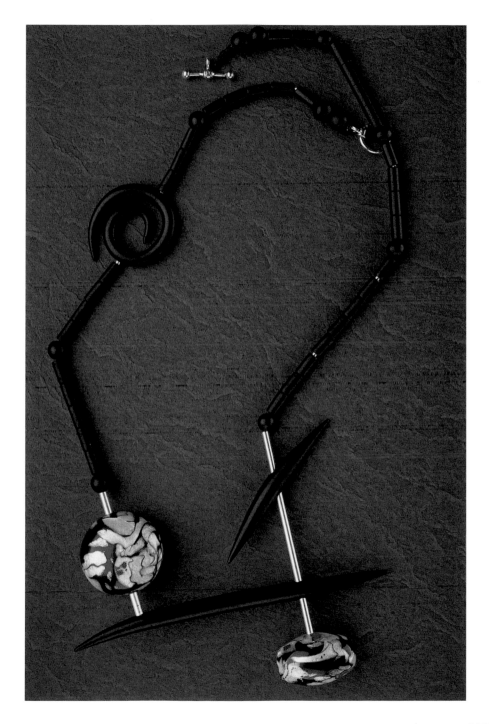

MAJ-BRITT CAWTHON

Swirl, 2001
28" (71.1 cm); round bead 1 ½" (3.8 cm)
Fimo; silver, silk tubing, silver toggle clasp
Photo by John Bonath, Maddog Studios

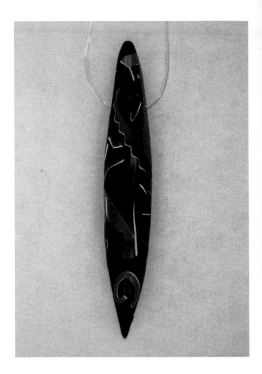

DOROTHY GREYNOLDS

Black Rainbow Bead, 2000
4 ½ x ¾ x ½" (11.4 x 1.9 x 1.3 cm)
Premo!; Skinner blend
Photo by artist

JENNIFER BEZINGUE

Under the Deep Blue Sea Beads, 2002
1 ½" (3.8 cm) diameter beads
Premo!; glitter, mica powders
Photo by Elizabeth Sloan

Layering translucent over metallic clay,
then sanding and polishing the cured
bead, results in a piece with glass-like
shine and heft. More than one lampwork
artist has complimented me on these
beads, only to be astonished that they
are made of polymer clay. *–JB*

KIM CAVENDER

Moondance, 2002
5 ½ x 5 ½ x ¼" (14 x 14 x .6 cm)
Kato Polyclay; embossing powder, wood; textured,
canework, press molded
Photo by Cam Harmon

KAREN MITCHELL

La Borsa Di Blu (The Blue Purse), 1997
9 ¾ x 5 ½ x ¼" (24.7 x 14 x .6 cm)
Translucent Liquid Sculpey, Premo!; silk
organza and taffeta, embroidery thread,
thread, wire, glass seed beads, crystal
beads, glass stones, silver metallic leaf, oil
paint, PearlEx powder, varnish; appliqué,
millefiori, impression glazed, hand and
machine stitched

Photo by Ai Buangsuwon

HARRIET SMITH

Triangle Box, 2002
6 x 6 x 6" (15.2 x 15.2 x 15.2 cm)
Polymer clay

KATHLEEN DUSTIN

Madonna Evening Purse, 2000
7 x 7 x 4" (17.5 x 17.5 x 10.2 cm)
Premo!, Sculpey III, liquid polymer; colored
pencil, gold leaf, Viton rubber handle; multiple
layering and baking, sanded, polished
Photo by George Post

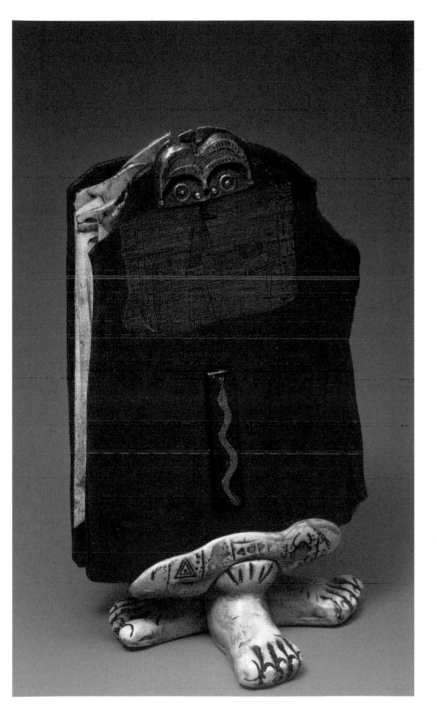

DAYLE DOROSHOW

Egyptian Spell Book, 2002
6 x 3 x 2" (15.2 x 7.5 x 5.1 cm)
Fimo; transferred image, found metal; carved, stamped
Photo by Don Felton

Inspired by the artifacts of Egypt and early hieroglyphics,
this book opens to reveal polymer pages of designs and
poetry from ancient Egypt. *—DD*

BONNIE BISHOFF
J.M. SYRON

Star Chair, 2002
30 x 30 x 23" (76.2 x 76.2 x 58.6 cm)
Premo!; figured cherry, faux leather;
veneered
Photo by Dean Powell

Exquisite craftsmanship is evident in
this combination of caneworked
polymer clay and fine woodworking.
Especially intriguing is the subtle color
reversal employed in the polymer clay
designs. *–ISD*

HARRIET SMITH

Pyramid Boxes, 2002
6 x 6 x 7" (15.2 x 15.2 x 17.5 cm)
Polymer clay

SYNDEE HOLT

Flame Flower, 2002
5 x 8 x 1" (12.7 x 20.3 x 2.5 cm)
Premo!
Photo by artist

VICKI RHINE

Sundance, 1993
12 x 5 ½ x ½" (30.5 x 14 x 1.3 cm)
Premo!; twigs, wire, PearlEx powders;
millefiori, stamped
Photo by Randy Ada

BONNIE BISHOFF
J.M. SYRON

Woodland Secrets (Wall-Hung Cabinet), 1999
34 x 26 x 12" (86.4 x 66.1 x 30.5 cm)
Premo!; mahogany, tiger maple, bird's-eye maple,
glass shelves, halogen light fixture; veneered
Photo by Dean Powell

JUDY KUSKIN

Untitled (Bracelet), 2003
8 x 1 x ¼" (20.3 x 2.5 x .6 cm)
Premo!, Fimo, Precious Metal Clay; fine and sterling silver
Photo by Penina Meisels

DEBORAH KILE

Brooch with Display Stand, 2002
6 ¾ x 5 ¼ x 2 ½" (17.1 x 13.1 x 6.3 cm)
Premo!; aluminum, solder, silver, aluminum
screen; stamped
Photo by artist

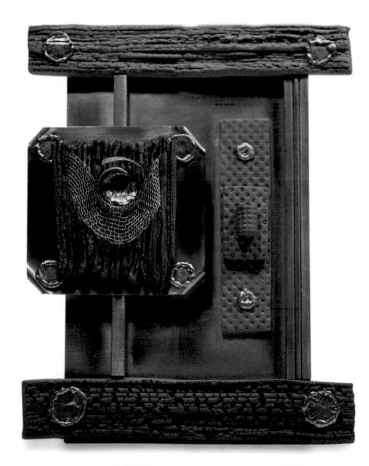

PETE JIRLES

Four Horsemen: Greed, 2000
9 x 6 x 6" (22.9 x 15.2 x 15.2 cm)
Sculpey SuperFlex; acrylic paint, African padauk
Photo by artist

This skillfully sculpted figure uses line and
movement to effectively convey convincing qualities
of vitality and realism. *–ISD*

LAURA TIMMINS

Ocean Flower, 2002
11 x 10 x 5" (27.9 x 25.4 x 12.7 cm)
Premo!; glass beads, wire-mesh armature
Photo by artist

The surreal underwater scenery of the tropics
was the inspiration for this piece. *–LT*

WENDY WALLIN MALINOW

Spring Shoe, 1999
10 ½ x 4 x 2 ½" (26.7 x 10.2 x 6.3 cm)
Polymer clay; telephone wire
Photo by Courtney Frisse

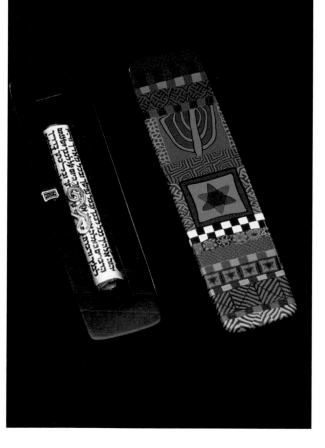

SUE FLEISCHER

SP Mezzuzah, 2002
4 x 1 x ¾" (102 x 2.5 x 1.9 cm)
Polymer clay; silver; millefiori
Photo by David Egan

ANNIE M.

Botanical Heart, 2000
1 ¾ x 1 ¼ x ¼" (4.4 x 3.2 x .6 cm)
Fimo
Photo by Jerry Anthony

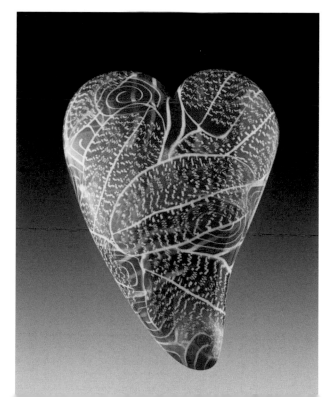

VIRGINIA V. SPERRY

Orange Flower Basket, 2001
7 x 5 ½" (17.5 x 14 cm)
Fimo; steel wire; rolled, millefiori
Photo by Herrmann/Starke

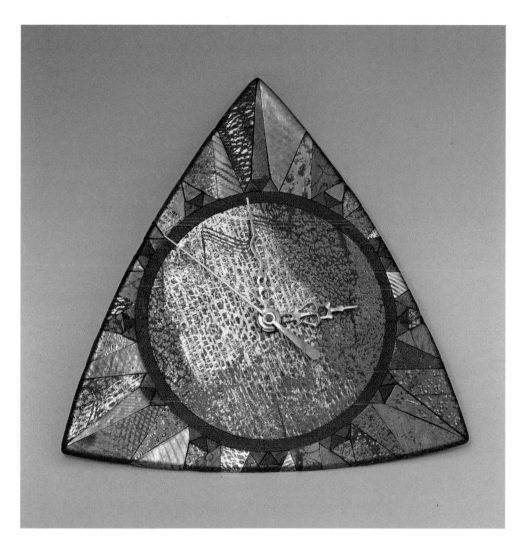

LINDA GOFF

Speckled Clock, 2003
8 x 8 x 1" (20.3 x 20.3 x 2.5 cm)
Polymer clay; clock parts, foils, metallic leaf
Photo by Daniel S. Kapsner

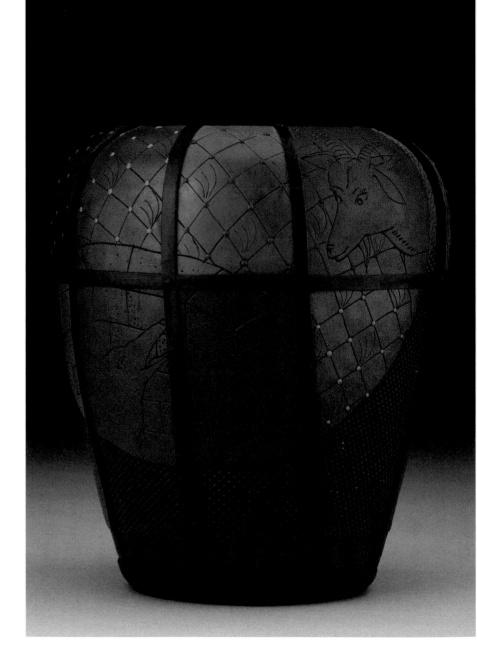

MAGGIE MAGGIO

Tit For Tat Fable Vessel, 1996
9 x 7 x 7" (22.9 x 17.5 x 17.5 cm)
Polymer clay
Photo by Bill Bachuber

All my fable vessels were inspired by the
character of the fox in Aesop's Fables. *Tit
For Tat* comes from the story of the fox and
the goat. *–MM*

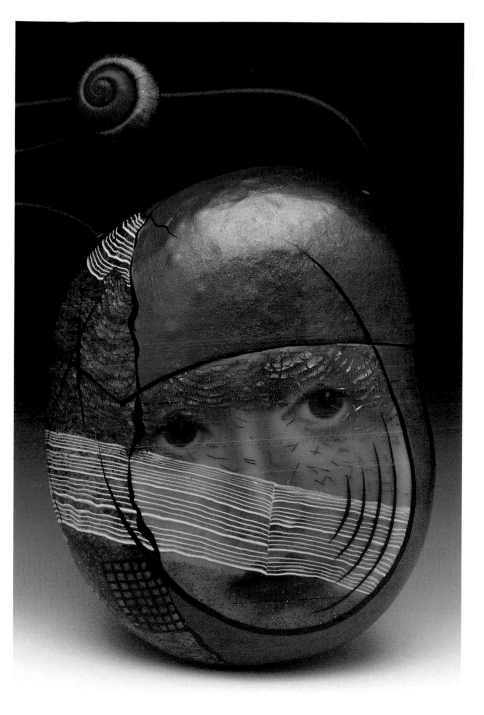

KATHLEEN DUSTIN

Polished Face Evening Purse, 2002
6 x 5 x 3" (15.2 x 12.7 x 7.5 cm)
Premo!, Sculpey III, liquid polymer; colored
pencil, gold leaf, Viton rubber handle;
layered, sanded, polished
Photo by George Post

PAM WYNN

Wow, 2002
2 x 5 x 2" (5.1 x 12.7 x 5.1 cm)
Premo!; Swarovski crystal head pins, gold-filled wire,
expansion bracelet
Photo by Meredith Hartsfield

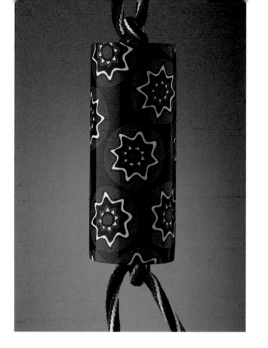

DIANE W. VILLANO

Big Bead–African Trade Bead, 2003
6 x 2 ½ x 2 ½" (15.2 x 6.3 x 6.3 cm)
Premo!; chipboard, kumihlmo cord
Photo by Harold Shapiro

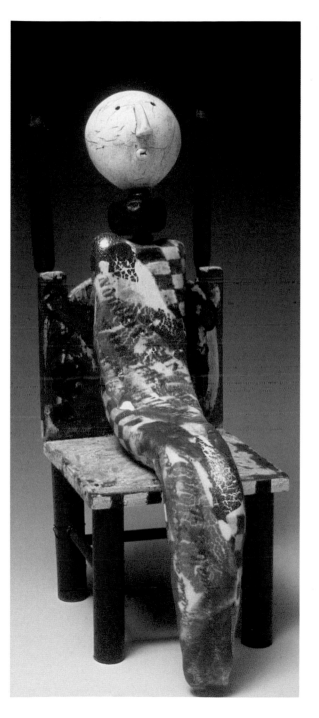

DAYLE DOROSHOW

The Wishing Chair, 2002
12 x 4 x 6" (30.5 x 10.2 x 15.2 cm)
Fimo; transferred image, gold leaf, patina; sculpted
Photo by Don Felton

Dayle Doroshow uses a variety of techniques and mixed media to create work
with spiritual significance and hidden messages. –ISD

JEAN COHEN

Wise Woman, 2002
4 ½ x 2 ½ x 1 ¼" (11.4 x 6.3 x 3.2 cm)
Polymer clay; bone fish, bone beads, gold
beads, rubber cord, metal hinges,
transferred image; embossed
Photo by Norman Watkins

I find myself drawn to pieces that have
hidden spaces. The Oriental woman
hiding her face with a fan suggested to
me that there is more than meets the
eye, which happens again on the inside
of the lid. –JC

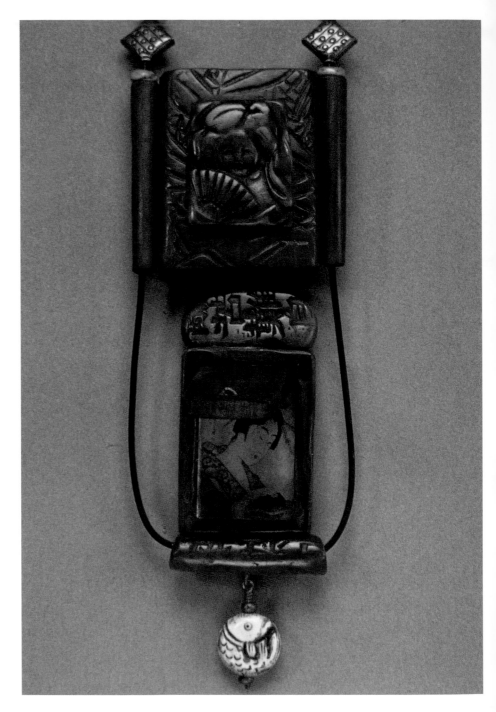

MAGS BONHAM

Mt. Fuji, 2002
2 ¼ x 2 ½ x ¾" (5.7 x 6.3 x 1.9 cm)
Premo!, Translucent Liquid Sculpey; PearlEx powders, watch face,
transferred image, glass and metal beads, nylon cording, bead
thread; rubber stamped
Photo by Jeff Clark

I'm inspired by ancient Japanese Inro. To give my pendants a more
modern function, I've added watch faces. *–MB*

DESIREE MCCROREY

Sparkling Moss Agate Beads, 2001–2002
Largest 3 x ¾ x ¾" (7.5 x 1.9 x 1.9 cm)
Polymer clay; PearlEx powders; rolled,
carved, sanded, polished
Photo by Liv Ames

CYNTHIA TOOPS

Rolodex Series: Ikat, 2002
1 ¼ x 3 ½ x 3 ½" (3.2 x 8.8 x 8.8 cm)
Polymer clay; steel spring
Photo by Roger Schreiber

MARY FILAPEK
LOU ANN TOWNSEND

Personal Orbit, 2003
6 x 5 ½ x ⅝" (15.2 x 14 x 1.6 cm)
Polymer clay; sterling silver, black onyx, stainless steel cable
Photo by Margot Geist

JAMES LEHMAN

Mostly Green and Red, 2002
5 ½ x 13 ½ x 13 ½" (14 x 34.3 x 34.3 cm)
Premo!, Sculpey III; wood, polyurethane; sanded
Photo by artist

GWEN GIBSON

Wearable Vessel, 2003
2 ¼ x 1 ½ x 1" (5.7 x 3.8 x 2.5 cm)
Premo!; acrylic paint; embossed
Photo by Robert Diamante

PEG GERARD

Turtle Necklace, 1998
2 ½ x 6 x ½" (6.3 x 15.2 x 1.3 cm)
Fimo; silver and gold metallic foil; canework
Photo by Pat Berrett

TAMELA WELLS LAITY

One, 2003
6 x 5 x 1 ½" (15.2 x 12.7 x 3.8 cm)
Premo!, Precious Metal Clay; silver leaf,
paste paper, stone, wood
Photo by Tim Barnwell

NANCY POLLACK

Floating Necklace, 2002
14 x 2 ½ x ¼" (35.6 x 6.3 x .6 cm)
Premo!; gold-filled beads, sterling silver wire, rubber
Buna cord, acrylic paint, varnish
Photo by Norman Watkins

PAT PETTYJOHN

Trumpet Flower, 2003
3 ½ x 2 x 1 ½" (8.8 x 5.1 x 3.8 cm)
Premo!; gold leaf, sterling silver
Photo by John Lucas

I had a different design in mind that didn't
work out. When I started to crumple the
piece on my scrap pile, I noticed a nice
shape and it took off from there. Many of my
pieces happen when I'm not even trying!

–PP

KATHLEEN BOLAN

Kuren (Crane), 2003
7 ½ x 1 ¼" (19 x 3.2 cm)
Fimo, Precious Metal Clay; sterling silver,
22k gold leaf, acrylic paints, photocopied
and transferred image; silkscreened,
molded, rubber stamped
Photo by Tim Thayer

ANDRÉE CHÉNIER

Elf of the Court #1, 2003
3 x 3 x 3" (7.5 x 7.5 x 7.5 cm)
Sculpey SuperFlex, Premo!, Fimo; wire armature, paint
Photo by Steve Mann

VIRGINIA V. SPERRY

Self Portrait, 2002
6 x 9" (15.2 x 22.9 cm)
Fimo; pastel paper, frame; millefiori
Photo by artist

This caneworked self-portrait by Virginia Sperry
illustrates convincing dimension and amazing
shadow and light play. *–ISD*

KRISTA WELLS

Zentrifugal Force, 2002
4 ¾ x 17 x ½" (12.1 x 43.2 x 1.3 cm)
Premo!, Fimo; glass beads, wire, acrylic paint; textured
Photo by Julian Beveridge

LAURIE MIKA

Mosaic Table, 2002
20 x 12 x 12" (50.8 x 30.5 x 30.5 cm)
Sculpey; acrylic paint, varnish, glaze
Photo by artist

This mosaic-style tabletop was
created with my own unique
handmade tiles (my claim to fame!).
Using white regular Sculpey, rolling it
out and cutting tiles, I then hand-
paint each one—I love the look when
it's finished because it's something
that can't be achieved using standard
mosaic techniques. *–LM*

BONNIE BISHOFF
J.M. SYRON

Java Credenza, 2001
38 x 56 x 24" (96.5 x 142.2 x 61 cm)
Premo!; mahogany, pommele sapeli; veneered
Photo by Dean Powell

SANDRA McCAW

Snowbird, 2001
2 x 2 ½ x ¹⁄₁₆" (5.1 x 6.3 x .2 cm)
Polymer clay
Photo by Jeff Baird

ELISE WINTERS

Dance of Life Necklace I, 2002
20" (50.8 cm)
Fimo, Premo!; 14k gold foil, crazed acrylic
Photo by Ralph Gabriner

GERRI NEWFRY

Alone Mini Book Amulet, 2002
36" (91.4 cm); amulet 2 ½ x 1 ½ x .¼"
 (6.3 x 3.8 x .6 cm)
Premo!; archival papers, beads,
beading thread, wire; mokume gane,
rubber stamped
Photo by Larry Sanders

KARYN KOZAK

Teapot, 2002
6 x 7 x 1 ¼" (15.2 x 17.5 x 3.2 cm)
Fimo; porcelain armature; millefiori, sanded, polished
Photo by Ryell Ho

JOANNE BAÑUELOS

Muerto Beauties, 2002
Larger 5 x 3 x 2 ¼" 12.7 x 7.5 x 5.7 cm)
Fimo; acrylic paints
Photo by Liv Ames

I love the images of skeletons and devils displayed during the Mexican holiday called *Dias de los Muertos* (Days of the Dead). They're not morbid, but instead exhibit a sense of humor. *—JB*

JENNIFER BEZINGUE

Mosaic Box, 2001
4 ½ x 5 x 4" (11.4 x 12.7 x 10.2 cm)
Premo!, Translucent Liquid Sculpey; glass beads;
textured, mica shift technique, inlaid beadwork
Photo by Elizabeth Sloan

The combination of techniques creates a rich
field of texture that is kept in check by the
limited color palette. –JB

GINNIE PARRISH

Handful of Stars, 2003
Premo!; mirror, costume jewelry, beads, wire,
acrylic fingernails; millefiori
Photo by Ron Tomlinson

HARRIET SMITH

Heart Box, 2002
6 x 6 x 6" (15.2 x 15.2 x 15.2 cm)
Polymer clay
Photo by Eugenia Uhl

KIM CAVENDER

Art Clock #6, 2002
5 ½ x 5 ½ x ¼" (14 x 14 x .6 cm)
Kato Polyclay; metallic leaf, oil paint, wood; stamped
Photo by Cam Harmon

JEFFREY LLOYD DEVER

Companions–Single-Wall Seaform Box with Attached Hollow Forms, 2003
2 ¾ x 2 ¾ x 6 ½" (7 x 7 x 16.5 cm)
Polymer clay; glass pin bead
Photo by Gregory R. Staley

Jeff Dever uses vibrant, complementary color pairings and interesting surface
textures, including piercing, to create his fanciful organic forms. *–ISD*

JUDY BELCHER

Whimsical Handbag, 2003
6 ½ x 7 x 3" (16.5 x 17.5 x 7.5 cm)
Kato Polyclay; cotton cording
Photo by Steve Payne

This handbag is stitched entirely on a
sewing machine. The draped scarf is also
of polymer clay. –JB

KATHY SHIELD

Annie's Treasure Box, 2002
3 ³⁄₈ x 5 ³⁄₄" (8.6 x 14.6 cm)
Polymer clay
Photo by artist

JULIA CONVERSE SOBER

Chromatic Cylinder Vessel, 2002
8 x 2 ½" (20.3 x 6.3 cm)
Premo!, Translucent Liquid Sculpey; colored pencil, silver leaf; pencil transfer
Photo by Larry Sanders

Transfers made using liquid clay are quite strong and flexible, so I've experimented with applying them to curved surfaces. For this box, I wrapped a single transfer around a pre-baked form and secured it in place with additional strips of clay. The contrast between matte black clay and brilliant color, the underlying glow of silver leaf highlighting texture, and the smooth, shiny surface of the transfer give this piece a jewel-like quality. *–JCS*

JEAN COHEN

Attitude, 2002
6 ½ x 5 x 1 ½" (16.5 x 12.7 x 3.8 cm)
Polymer clay; gold leaf, PearlEx powders,
gold trim, metal hinge
Photo by Norman Watkins

I like the idea of a functional object made
from a non-functional material. I'm also
excited that the teapot lid can be worn as a
pin—a surprise when you first see it. *–JC*

KATHLEEN BOLAN

Shiawase: Happiness, 2003
2 ¾ x 2 ¼" (7 x 5.7 cm)
Fimo, Precious Metal Clay; sterling silver, 22k gold leaf,
photocopied and transferred image; rubber stamped
Photo by Tim Thayer

This piece is mounted on sterling silver hooks in an
11 x 14-inch frame, so it can be displayed when it's
not being worn as jewelry. –KB

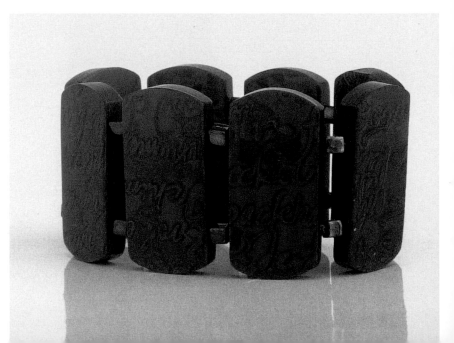

KAREN WOODS

Two-Sided Bracelet, 2002
1 ½ x 4" (3.8 x 10.2 cm)
Polymer clay; glass beads; textured,
mokume gane, rubber stamped

NAN ROCHE

Lotus, 2002
3 ½ x 3 ½ x ½" (8.8 x 8.8 x 1.3 cm)
Polymer clay; layered, press molded, sanded, polished
Photo by artist

KATHLEEN DUSTIN

Women of the Harem Neckpiece, 1997
Figures 6 ½" (16.5 cm)
Premo!; millefiori
Photo by George Post

CHRISTINE DICKERSON

Stormy Windows, 2002
28" (71.1 cm); 1 ½" (3.8 cm) beads
Premo!; canework
Photo by Karen Carter

SUE SMITH

Antipodean Wave, 2003
4 ¾ x 1 ½ x 3 ⅛" (12 x 4 x 8 cm)
Fimo; sterling silver

PATRICIA KIMLE

Feathered Egg, Box and Pendant, 2001
6 x 3 x 3" (15.2 x 7.5 x 7.5 cm)
Premo!; goose egg, leafing, paints, 14k gold
chain; carved
Photo by artist

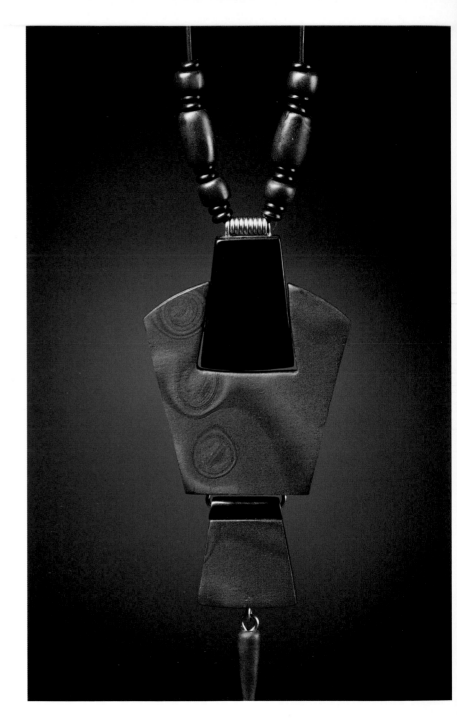

PAT PETTYJOHN

Seeing Red, 2003
4 ½ x 2 ¼ x ¼"
Premo!; sterling silver, Buna cord
Photo by John Lucas

PATRICIA KIMLE

Circles in Pieces, 2001
22 x 1 ½ x ³⁄₈" (55.9 x 3.8 x .9 cm)
Premo!; gold leaf, tiger eye, 14k gold beads;
mica shift technique
Photo by artist

DOROTHY GREYNOLDS

Rainforest Beads, 2003
2 ¼ x 1 ⅛ x ⅜" (5.7 x 2.8 x .9 cm)
Premo!; rubber stamped, textured, layered,
Skinner blend
Photo by artist

CLARE BALOMBIN

Fuschia Purse, 2001
2 ⅛ x 4 ¼ x 1" (5.4 x 10.8 x 2.5 cm)
Premo!; variegated gold and silver leaf, acrylic
paint, satin cord
Photo by Karen Carter

ELISE WINTERS

Cinched Brooch, 2002
4 x ½ x ½" (10.2 x 1.3 x 1.3 cm)
Fimo, Premo!; vermeil, crazed acrylic
Photo by Ralph Gabriner

RACHEL GOURLEY

Rock Boxes, 2002
2 x 3" (5.1 x 7.5 cm)
Fimo, Premo!, Liquid Sculpey
Photo by Michael Decourcy

DARIA KOLATALO

Untitled, 2003
3 x 4 x 4" (7.5 x 10.2 x 10.2 cm)
Premo!
Photo by Howard Marr

EMILY S. RIGELSKY

The Confrontation, 2002
5 ½ x 18 x 7" (14 x 45.7 x 17.5 cm)
Sculpey SuperFlex; glass eyes, acrylic paints
Photo by Jason Kotte

Two gryphons protect their nest of eggs from a black dragon bent
on revenge. This is one of my largest pieces. Each scale and
feather are individually sculpted, and the base is fully textured.

—ESR

KATHERINE DEWEY

After the Hunt, 2002
5 x 4 x 4" (12.7 x 10.2 x 10.2 cm)
Premo!, Sculpey SuperFlex; brass wire and
mat-board armature, water-based oil paint,
acrylic varnish, PearlEx powders; carved,
hand etched, rubbed
Photo by Chase Fountain

The bow, made of polymer clay over a
piano wire armature and strung with
button thread, really works. *–KD*

BARBARA VAN NOY

The Gift Giver, 2000
25 x 12 x 12" (63.5 x 30.5 x 30.5 cm)
ProSculpt; musical base, antique book
Photo by Mark Wright, Rockafellow Photography

DEBRA DE WOLFF

Bracelet, 2003
7 ³⁄₈ x 2 ¹⁄₄" (18.4 x 5.7 cm)
Polymer clay; seed beads, glass, sterling magnetic clasp
Photo by Maria Ellen Huebner

Bright colors, fun shapes, and playful textures energize
Debra De Wolff's modern bracelet design. *–ISD*

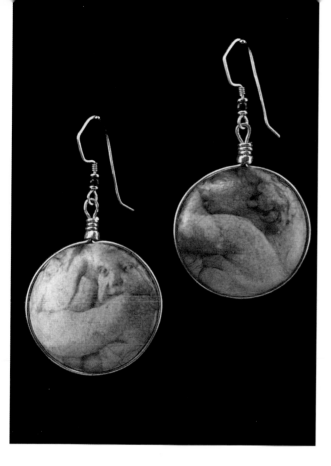

CHRISTOPHER KNOPPEL

Emulsion Transfer Earrings, 2002
1 ½ x 2 ½" (3.8 x 6.3 cm)
Fimo, Translucent Liquid Sculpey; sterling silver
wire wrap and ear wire, seed beads, transferred
photographic emulsion
Photo by Don Felton

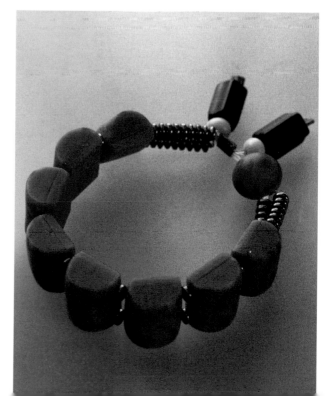

CHRISTINA KNAPP

Coral-like Bracelet, 2003
⅝ x 7 ¼ x ⅜" (1.6 x 18.7 x .9 cm)
Fimo; hematite, bone and glass beads,
clear elastic, brass tubes
Photo by artist

MARGARET M. CANAVAN

Jungle Blossom, 2003
3 ½ x 4 ½ x 4 ½" (8.8 x 11.4 x 11.4 cm)
Fimo, Translucent Liquid Sculpey; glass seed beads
Photo by artist

MARY GRANDY

Flowers on My Heart, 2002
8 ¼ x 10 x 1 ⅛" (21 x 25.4 x 2.9 cm)
Fimo; mirror, glue
Photo by artist

JULIA CONVERSE SOBER

Triangular Lantern Earrings, 2003
2 ½ x ¾ x ¾" (6.3 x 1.9 x 1.9 cm)
Premo!, Precious Metal Clay; microscope
slides, metal tubing, gold-filled beads and
wire, rubber O-rings; canework
Photo by Larry Sanders

The organic quality of the translucent
canework complements these geometric
shapes of glass and metal. Julia Sober
thinks beyond the polymer clay and
focuses on form and construction in these
finely crafted earrings. *–ISD*

MARGARET REGAN

Stick Pin Duo, 2002
3 x 1 x ½" (7.5 x 2.5 x 1.3 cm)
Polymer clay; nickel silver, sterling silver
Photo by George Post

RACHEL CARREN

Leaf Bracelet, 2003
1 ½ x 2 ½ x 2 ½" (3.8 x 6.3 x 6.3 cm)
Premo!; metal leaf; stamped
Photo by Ralph Gabriner

The simple shape of this bracelet is the perfect vehicle for the rich, multi-layered surface treatment in this elegant design. *–ISD*

DEBRA DEMBOWSKI

Bird Lady, 2001
5 x 2 ¾" (12.7 x 7 cm)
Premo!; acrylic paint, beads, sterling silver; mokume gane
Photo by Larry Sanders

LAURA TIMMINS

Pendant, 2003
2 x 1 ½ x ½" (5.1 x 3.8 x 1.3 cm)
Premo!; glitter
Photo by artist

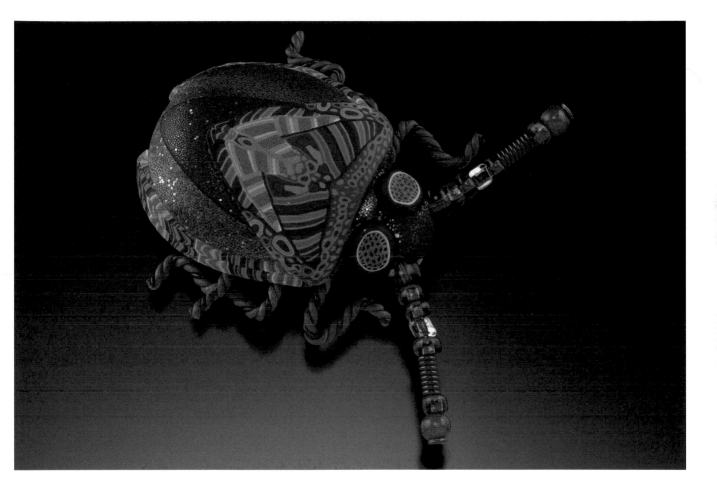

JOYCE FRITZ

Beetle Pin, 2003
2 x 1 ½ x ¾" (5.1 x 3.8 x 1.9 cm)
Fimo; recycled telephone wire, glass beads, niobium coils, glitter
Photo by Larry Sanders

JUDY S. BELCHER

Wild Women, 2002
7 ¾ x ¼ x ⅛" (19.7 x .6 x .3 cm)
Fimo; seed beads, metal toggle clasp
Photo by Steve Payne

ALISON CURTIN

Happy Girls Bracelet, 2000
8 x ¾" (20.3 x 1.9 cm)
Polymer clay; seed beads, glass beads
Photo by Karen Carter-The Image Factory

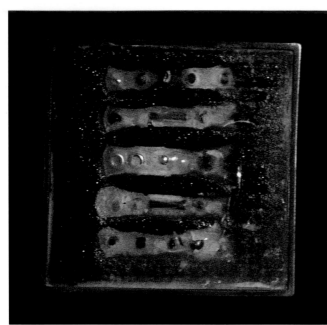

MARGARET KRISTOF

Mysterium Series, 1999
1 ¼ x 1 ¼" (3.2 x 3.2 cm)
Polymer clay; seed beads, origami paper, paint, brass bezel
Photo by Pad McLauglin

The surface of each pin is a cross-section of the original piece. Layers were baked, then cut down to reveal the center that lies within, revealing the mystery of each pin.
–MK

LENORA KANDINER

Snakeskin Necklace, 2001
4 ½ x 12" (11.4 x 30.5 cm)
Premo!; Buna cord
Photo by artist

JACQUELINE LEE

Egyptian Supplicant, 2000
1 ⅝ x 1 ¼ x ⅛" (4.1 x 3.2 x .3 cm)
Premo!; acrylic paints
Photo by Sherri Haab

NANCY POLLACK

Tree Vase, 2002
4 ½ x 2 ¾ x 2 ¼" (11.4 x 7 x 5.7 cm)
Premo!
Photo by Norman Watkins

Many times I mix up a sheet of clay with a
definite project in mind, then I discover that
the sheet disagrees with me and I must make
something else. Polymer clay work is about
waiting to see what will show up. *–NP*

DEBBIE NEIS

Patty's Box, 2003
5 x 3 ¾ x 3 ½" (12.7 x 9.4 x 8.8 cm)
Premo!; acrylic paints; rubber stamped
Photo by artist

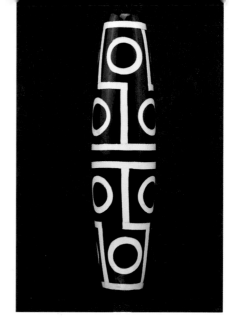

DIANE W. VILLANO

Big Bead–Inlaid Dzi Bead, 2001
6 ¼ x 1 ¼ x 1 ¼" (15.8 x 3.2 x 3.2 cm)
Premo¡ wood
Photo by William K. Sacco

SALLY SEILLER

Poppy Jar, 2001
4 ½ x 2 ¼" (11.4 x 5.7 cm)
Premo!; acrylic paint glaze, metallic wax
Photo by Third Eye Gallery, Helena MT

239

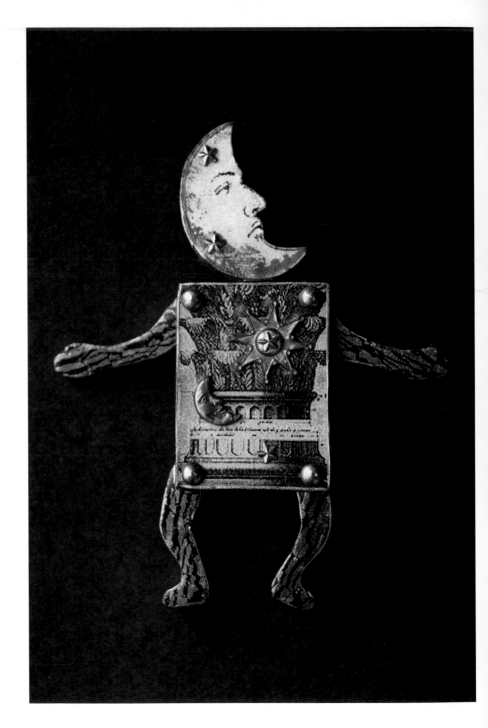

STEPHANIE JONES RUBIANO

Moon in the Man, 2002
¼ x 2 ½ x 3 ¾" (.6 x 6.3 x 9.4 cm)
Premo!; gold leaf, brass charms,
transferred image
Photo by artist

WENDY WALLIN MALINOW

Coral Mask, 2002
12 x 7 ½ x 2 ½" (30.5 x 19 x 6.3 cm)
Polymer clay; shells, pearls, wire, decorative ribbons
Photo by Courtney Frisse

This mask is what I like to think a mermaid might
wear to a watery masquerade party. *–WWM*

DEBRA DEMBOWSKI

Glamor Girl, 2001
5 x 3" (12.7 x 7.5 cm)
Premo!; acrylic paint, beads, sterling silver;
mokume gane
Photo by Larry Sanders

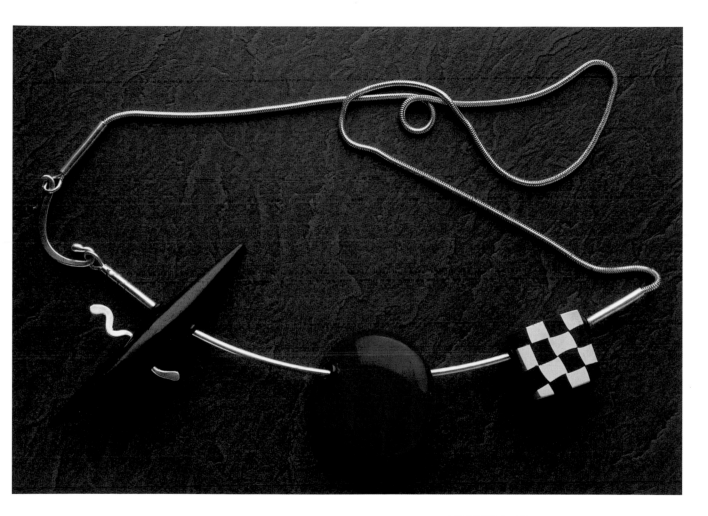

MAJ-BRITT CAWTHON

Checkerboard, 2002
26" (66 cm); sphere 1 ¾" (4.4 cm) diameter
Fimo; silver tube, silver snake chain and clasp
Photo by John Bonath, Maddog Studios

LAURA MEHR

Happenstance Boxes, 2002
Larger 10 x 3 x 3" (25.4 x 7.5 x 7.5 cm)
Premo!; lathe turned
Photo by Stuart Sklar

The removable heads on these boxes
can be worn as pins. –LM

KATHY SHIELD

Chinese Checkers Board, 2003
14 ½ x 16 ½" (36.8 x 41.9 cm)
Polymer clay; PearlEx powders; stenciled
Photo by artist

LAURIE MIKA

The Only Journey, 2002
10 x 8 x ½" (25.4 x 20.3 x 1.3 cm)
Premo!, Sculpey; PearlEx powders, jewelry
pieces, map pins; tessarae, rubber stamped
Photo by artist

This icon is the first piece in which I
experimented with polymer clay using
PearlEx powders and rubber stamps. I was
trying to achieve a piece that appeared
raku-fired. (I think it worked!) It was also
the first icon I've created by using the
fabulous stamps from Zettiology. –LM

JAMES LEHMAN

Spore, 2002
28 ½ x 11" (72.4 x 27.9)
Premo!, Sculpey III; finished with water-based
polyurethane hardwood floor finish
Photo by artist

TERRY LEE CZECHOWSKI

In Stall, 2002
8 x 10 x ¾" (20.3 x 25.4 x 1.9 cm)
Premo!; Lazertran image transfer, pastels
Photo by artist

MARISOL ROSS

The Short-Stop Diner, 2002
11 x 14 x 1 ¼" (27.9 x 35.6 x 3.2 cm)
Sculpey, Translucent Liquid Sculpey; mosaic grout,
colored pencil, acrylic paint, pine board
Photo by Peter Jacobs

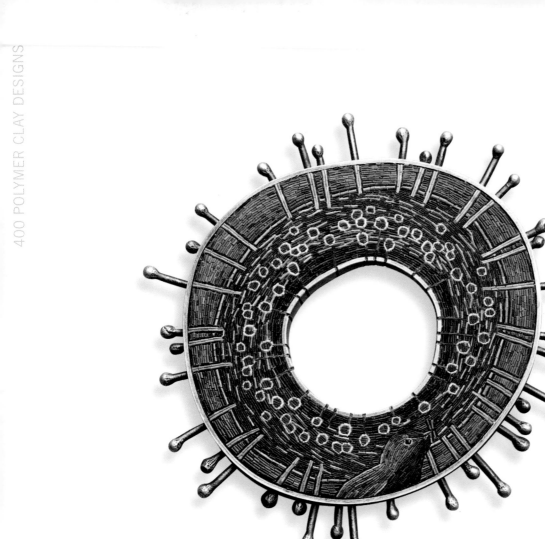

CYNTHIA TOOPS
CHUCK DOMITROVICH

3 ½ x 3 ¾ x ¼" (8.8 x 9.4 x .6 cm)
Polymer clay
Jewelry by Chuck Domitrovich
Photo by Roger Schreiber

WENDY WALLIN MALINOW

I Want Candy, 2002
24" (61 cm)
Polymer clay, Precious Metal Clay; silver,
sterling silver
Photo by Courtney Frisse

JACQUELINE LEE

Bamboo Salamander Inro, 2000
2 1/8 x 1 1/4 x 5/8" (5.7 x 3.2 x 1.6 cm)
Premo!; cord, acrylic paint, gold leaf
Photo by Dan Haab

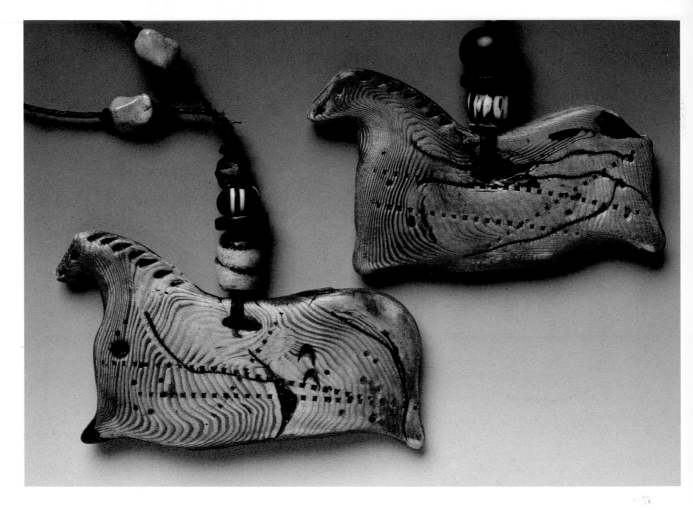

LUANN UDELL

Lascaux Horse Necklace, 2002
Larger 1 ½ x 2 x ¼" (3.8 x 5.1 x .6 cm)
Polymer clay
Photo by Jeff Baird

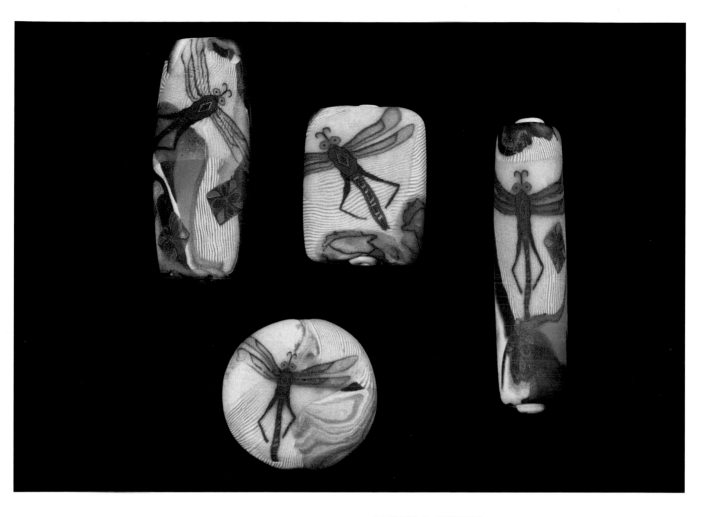

BARBARA A. MCGUIRE

Dragonfly Beads, 1997
1 x 3" (2.5 x 7.5 cm)
Polymer clay; canework
Photo by artist

LAURA TIMMINS

Bowl, 2002
5 x 12 x 12" (12.7 x 30.5 x 30.5 cm)
Polymer clay; hair, gold wire, paint, wire-mesh armature
Photo by artist

This bowl uses a spare, confident approach to surface design.
The highly tactile rim contrasts beautifully with its smooth
interior; the materials and colors suggest a tribal offering. *−ISD*

LAURA MEHR

Three-legged Necklace Receptacle, 2001
10 x 6 x 6" (25.4 x 15.2 x 15.2 cm)
Premo!; silk cord; millefiori, lathe turned
Photo by artist

JANE ZHAO

Two Chinese Dragons Play with the Ball, 2002
White: 12 x 5 x 8" (30.5 x 12.7 x 20.3 cm);
 Blue: 11 x 7 x 8 ¼" (27.9 x 17.8 x 20.7 cm)
Premo polymer clay; aluminum foil armature
Photo by Steve Mann

LAUREN ALEXANDER
CHERI HIERS

Teacup Faeries
Attacus Atlas Faerie, 2003
9 ½ x 7 x 5" (24.1 x 17.5 x 12.7 cm)
Polymer clay; porcelain, *attacus atlas* moth
wings, mohair, paper hat, felted shoes, wood
Photo by artist

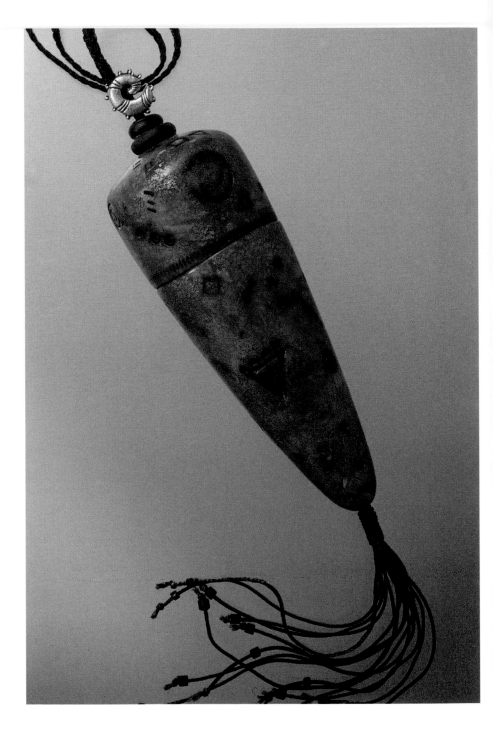

LAURA TABAKMAN

Vessel, 2002
3 x 1 x 1" (7.5 x 2.5 x 2.5 cm)
Premo!; braided cord, glass beads,
metallic foils, acrylic paint; stamped,
sanded, polished
Photo by artist

KATHLEEN DUSTIN

Red Apple on Granite–Evening Purse, 2003
5 x 6 x 4" (12.7 x 15.2 x 10.2 cm)
Premo!; embossing powders, brass chain
Photo by George Post

LORRAINE RANDECKER

Geometricks, 1999
17 x 2 ½" (43.2 x 6.3 cm)
Fimo
Photo by Mr. Randecker

MAGGIE MAGGIO

Sense of Place Necklace–Rainy Day Walk in the Autumn Woods of Mount Tabor, 2000
36" (91.4 cm)
Polymer clay; rubber cord
Photo by Bill Bachuber

HARRIET SMITH

Fishy Box, 2002
6 x 6 x 6" (15.2 x 15.2 x 15.2 cm)
Polymer clay

DIANE VILLANO

Miguel, 2003
6 ½ x 10 ¼ x 2 ½" (16.5 x 26 x 6.3 cm)
Premo!; papier-mâché
Photo by Harold Shapiro

CYNTHIA PACK

Chicken Legs Box, 2002
4 x 4 x 3" (10.2 x 10.2 x 7.6 cm)
Fimo; glass bead
Photo by Steve Mann

The box's coloring and thin legs were the deciding factors in choosing a name. Layering hundreds of little "feathers" can be quite time consuming, but the results are worth it. Translucent glass beads were added for contrast against the matte feathers. –CP

MICHELLE ROSS

"Soap Box" Box, 2003
3 ½ x 2 ⅞ x 1 ⅝" (8.8 x 7.2 x 4.1 cm)
Kato Polyclay; bar soap box, decorative paper,
transferred image; mokume gane, Skinner
blend, canework, textured
Photo by Cassy Muronaka

ANGIE WIGGINS

Tilted Chalice, 2002
8 ½ x 5 x 5" (21.6 x 12.7 x 12.7 cm)
Fimo; handmade paper, leather, glass beads,
metal; canework, surface texture, laminated
Photo by Steve Mann

MERRI BETH HILL

Roly Poly, 2000
7 x 3 ¾ x 3 ¼" (17.5 x 9.4 x 8.3 cm)
Fimo, Sculpey SuperFlex, ProMat;
brass bells, glass beads, acrylic paint
Photo by artist

KATHLEEN DUSTIN

Leaning Village Woman Purse, 2000
5 x 5 x 3" (12.7 x 12.7 x 7.5 cm)
Premo!, Sculpey III, liquid polymer; colored pencil, gold leaf;
layered, sanded, polished
Photo by George Post

JAMES LEHMAN

Post-Hypnotic Suggestion, 2001
6 ½ x 8 x 8" (16.5 x 20.3 x 20.3 cm)
Sculpey III; high-gloss varnish; sanded
Photo by artist

LAURA TIMMINS

Vessel, 2002
11 x 4 x 5" (27.9 x 10.2 x 12.7 cm)
Polymer clay; hair, paint, wire-mesh armature
Photo by artist

PORRO SAHLBERG

Disco Fossil, 2002
17 ¾ x 15 ¾ x ¼" (45 x 40 x .5 cm)
Premo!, Cernit; cotton thread, mica; molded
Photo by artist

JODY BISHEL

Moon Blossom Vessel, 1999
4 x 5 x 5" (10.2 x 12.7 x 12.7 cm)
Premo!, Translucent Liquid Sculpey; sea glass
Photo by Daniel Buckley

JUDY SUMMER

Patchwork, 2002
15 x 7 x 4 ½" (38.1 x 17.5 x 11.4 cm)
Premo!; wire armature with copper tubing and foil,
brass wire; canework
Photo by Debra Dietz

ANDRÉE CHÉNIER

"Wilbur"–Off-Duty Gargoyle #1, 2003
3 x 2 x 3 ½" (7.5 x 5.1 x 8.8 cm)
Sculpey SuperFlex, Sculpey, Translucent
Liquid Sculpey; wire armature, paint
Photo by artist

CYNTHIA TOOPS

Untitled, 2002
1 ½ x 3 ½ x 3 ½" (3.8 x 8.8 x 8.8 cm)
Fimo; steel springs
Photo by Roger Schreiber

I have always been interested in ethnic jewelry. In this piece, which is a part of my
Rolodex bracelet series, I wanted to create a tribal feel with a 21st-century material. –CT

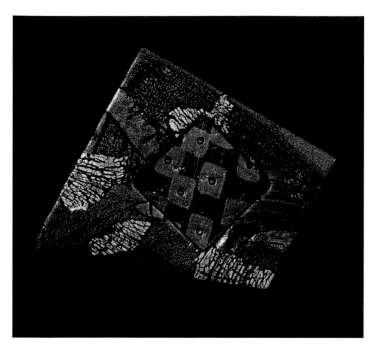

LISA WOLLMAN BOLICK

Brooch, 2002
2 ¾ x 2 ¼" (7 x 5.7 cm)
Premo!; acrylic paint, metallic pigment powders
Photo by artist

I'm a graphic designer so I'm influenced by my work with print design. My one-of-a-kind pieces tend to be graphic and geometric and employ both color and texture. –LWB

JILL ACKIRON-MOSES

Celebration Necklace, 2002–2003
18" (45.7 cm)
Premo!; acrylic paint, Swarovski crystals, glass beads, fiber, wire
Photo by Hap Sakwa

JANE ZHAO

Chinese Landscape, 2002
7 7/8 x 2 7/8 x 1/8" (20 x 7.2 x .3 cm)
Premo!; carved
Photo by Steve Mann

JAMES LEHMAN

Obviously, 2003
22 x 20 x 8" (55.9 x 50.8 x 20.3 cm)
Premo!, Sculpey III, Translucent Liquid
Sculpey; sanded
Photo by artist

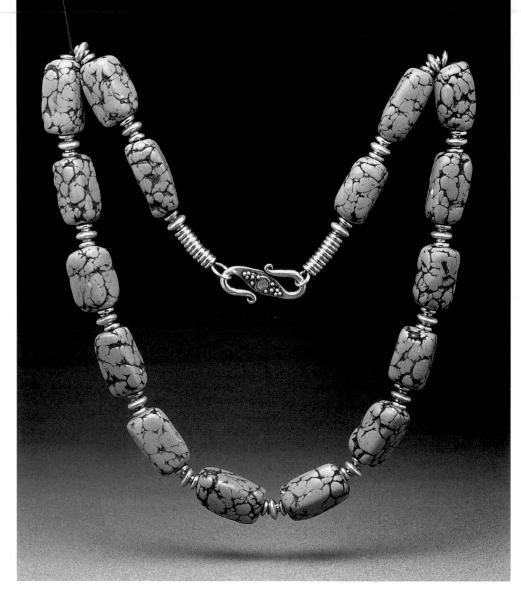

JEANETTE KANDRAY

Simply Turquoise, 2003
¾ x 25 x ¾" (1.9 x 63.5 x 1.9 cm)
Fimo; sterling silver beads and findings
Photo by Karen Carter

GWEN GIBSON

Kabuki, 2001
Each section 1 ¾ x 1" (4.4 x 2.5 cm); 2 ¼" (5.7 cm) inner diameter
Premo!; paint, elastic, transferred image
Photo by Robert Diamante

IRENE YURKEWYCH

Mica Shift Marquetry Vase, 2003
9 x 6 x 6" (22.9 x 15.2 x 15.2 cm)
Premo!; manipulated mica shift marquetry
Photo by Steve Mann

LINDA GOFF

Swirl Clock, 2003
8 x 8 x 1" (20.3 x 20.3 x 2.5 cm)
Polymer clay; clock parts, foils, metallic leaf
Photo by Daniel S. Kapsner

MONA KISSEL

Reversible Cuff Bracelet, 2003
1 ½ x 8 x ½" (3.8 x 20.3 x 1.3 cm)
Premo!; glass seed beads; rubber
stamped, textured
Photo by artist

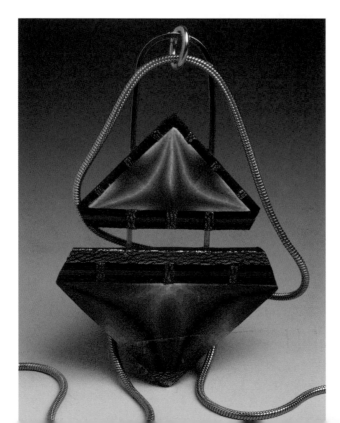

SANDRA McCAW

Untitled, 2002
3 x 2 x ⅛" (7.5 x 5.1 x .3 cm)
Fimo; gold-filled wire, 23k gold leaf
Photo by Jeff Baird

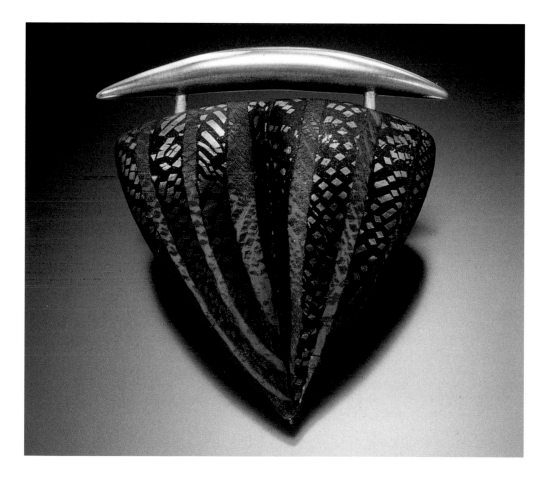

ELISE WINTERS

Lobed Brooch, 2002
1 ½ x 1 ½ x ⅜" (3.8 x 3.8 x .9 cm)
Fimo, Premo!; sterling silver, crazed acrylic
Photo by Ralph Gabriner

DEBBIE JACKSON

Jungle Reunion, 2002
5 x 8" (12.7 x 20.3 cm)
Fimo; cowrie shell; canework
Photo by Kojo Kamau

ANNABELLE FISHER

Black and White and Earth, 2000
3 x ⅞ x ⅛" (7.5 x 2.2 x .3 cm)
Fimo; millefiori
Photo by Jerry Anthony\

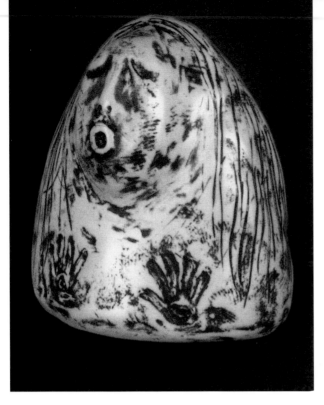

LILIAN CANOUET

Woman Spirit Rattle, 2001
2 x 1 ¾ x 1 ¼"
Fimo; acrylic paint; carved, stamped, rubbed
Photo by artist

DARIA KOLATALO

Untitled, 2002
3 x 4 x 4" (7.5 x 10.2 x 10.2 cm)
Sculpey Granitex; antiqued
Photo by Howard Marr

DEBBIE KRUEGER

Night & Day Necklace, 2002
32" (81.3 cm)
Polymer clay, Precious Metal Clay; silver and glass
beads; canework
Photo by George Post

DEBRA DEMBOWSKI

Dancer, 2001
4 ½ x 3" (11.4 x 7.5 cm)
Premo!; acrylic paint, beads, sterling silver
Photo by Larry Sanders

MARGARET FISCHER

Polyglow Neckpiece, 1997
28" (71.1 cm)
ProMat; silver and gold foil, beads
Photo by artist

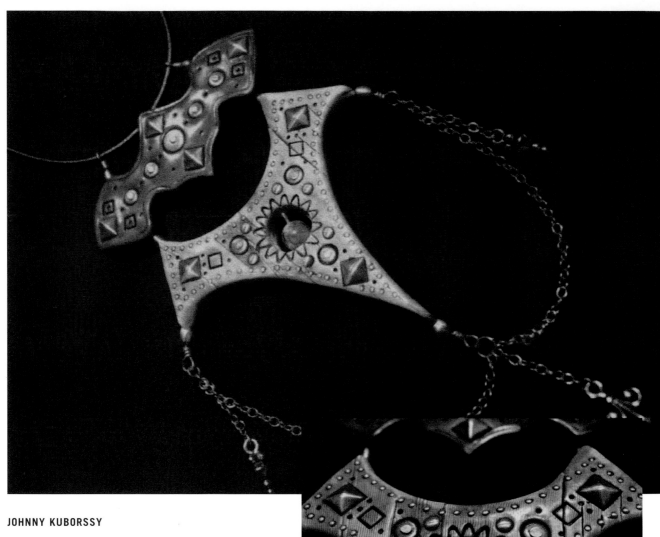

JOHNNY KUBORSSY

The Harem, 2003
5 x 2 ½ x ¼" (12.7 x 6.3 x .6 cm)
Premo!; jasper bead, fishing swivels, brass findings,
rubber cord, acrylic paint; etched
Photo by Jim Ciarico

BANKS!

Jacaranda, 2003
18" (45.7 cm)
Premo!
Photo by artist

CYNTHIA PACK

Petal Bowl, 2002
5 x 5 x 5" (12.7 x 12.7 x 12.7 cm)
Fimo
Photo by Steve Mann

RIVER LEIGH WOLFE

Echoes, 2002
1 ½ x ¾ x 32" (3.8 x 1.9 x 81.3 cm)
Premo!; bronze seed beads, woven nylon cord,
acrylics; silk-screened
Photo by Jerry Anthony

LAUREN ALEXANDER
CHERI HIERS

Teacup Faeries
Morpho Melenaus Faerie, 2000
6 x 7 x 7" (15.2 x 17.5 x 17.5 cm)
Polymer clay; mohair, butterfly wings,
porcelain cup and saucer
Photo by artist

CARISSA NICHOLS

Alligator Dumpling, 2002
3 ½ x 1 ½ x ¾" (8.8 x 3.8 x 1.9 cm)
Premo!; sterling silver wire, hollow bead
Photo by Russ Moore

RACHEL CARREN

Fish Brooch, 2002
2 ³⁄₈ x 1 ⁵⁄₈ x ¹⁄₈" (6 x 3.1 x .3 cm)
Polymer clay; photocopied transferred
image; imprinted, Skinner blend
Photo by Ralph Gabriner

1634
GWEN GIBSON

Flashy Cuff, 2002
1 ⁵⁄₈ x ¹⁄₂ x 2" (3.1 x 1.3 x 5.1 cm)
Premo!; acrylic paint; embossed
Photo by Robert Diamante

JUDY BELCHER

Violet Handbag, 2003
3 x 6 x 3" (7.5 x 15.2 x 7.5 cm)
Kato Polyclay; cotton cording
Photo by Steve Payne

This purse is sewn entirely on a sewing machine. –JB

LYNNE ANN SCHWARZENBERG

"Baroque Butterfly" Bottle of Hope, 2003
3 x 1 ¼ x 1 ¼" (7.5 x 3.2 x 3.2 cm)
Premo!; glass bottle, PearlEx powder; molded
Photo by Harold Shapiro

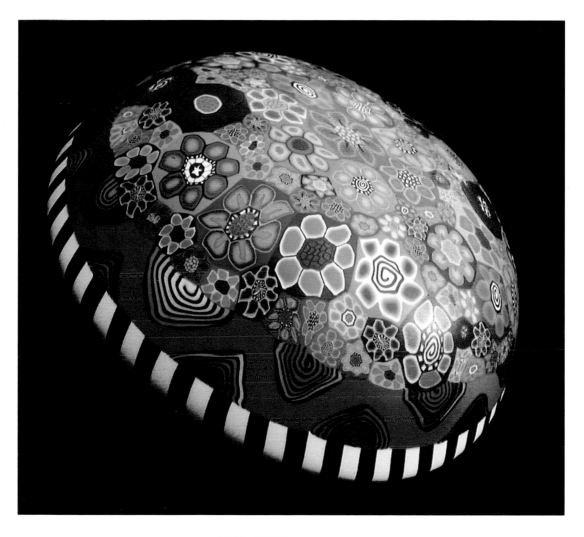

SUE FLEISCHER

Geo-Shade Flower Bowl, 2003
3 ¼ x 1 ¾" (8.3 x 4.4 cm)
Polymer clay; millefiori
Photo by artist

KLEW [KAREN LEWIS]

Drum Beat, 2002
1 ½ x ⅝" (3.8 x 1.6 cm)
Polymer clay
Photo by Marcia Albert

RIVER LEIGH WOLFE

One Fish-Two Fish, Yellow Fish-Blue Fish, 2003
2 x ½ x 32" (5.1 x 1.3 x 81.3 cm)
Premo!; 14k gold-filled wire, beads, tassel,
turquoise, coral, embossing powder, acrylics,
gold gel pen; silkscreened
Photo by Jerry Anthony

CAROLYN POTTER

Spirit, 2002
7 x 5 x 2 ½" (17.5 x 12.7 x 6.3 cm)
Sculpey, Premo!; acrylic paint, aluminum foil
armature; Skinner blend, press molded
Photo by Corie Photography

IRENE YURKEWYCH

Mica Shift Marquetry Box, 2002
3 x 4 x 4" (7.5 x 10.2 x 10.2 cm)
Premo!; manipulated mica shift marquetry
Photo by Steve Mann

311

BARBARA VAN NOY

The Dollmaker, 2000
18 x 16 x 16 ½" (46.2 x 40.6 x 41.9 cm)
ProSculpt; musical base
Photo by Mark Wright, Rockafellow Photography

All of my designs have hand-tied
eyelashes and dentures. *—BVN*

ROBERT WILEY

Faux Wood Necklace, 2002
12 x 4 x ⅜" (30.5 x 10.2 x .9 cm)
Premo!; inlay
Photo by George Post

JOANN BOYER

My Summer in the Garden, 2000
3 x 3 x ½" (7.5 x 7.5 x 1.3 cm)
Fimo; hemp twine hinges, photocopied transferred image,
acrylic paint; molded, rubber stamped
Photo by Al Boyer

DEBRA DE WOLFF

Collection of Bracelets, 2003
⅜ x 2 ¾" (.9 x 7 cm)
Polymer clay; seed beads
Photo by Maria Ellen Huebner

KAREN MITCHELL

Windows of India, 2001
19 x 13 x 8 ½" (48.3 x 33 x 21.6 cm)
Translucent Liquid Sculpey, Premo!;
polyester chiffon, metallic cord, thread,
glitter, oil paint, printed chiffon, hand-
colored and photocopied composite
transferred image; millefiori, punched,
machine stitched from original pattern
Photo by Steve Mann

ELISE WINTERS

Shell Earrings, 2002
1 ¼ x 1 x ½" (3.2 x 2.5 x 1.3 cm)
Fimo, Premo!; crazed acrylic
Photo by Ralph Gabriner

LIBBY MILLS

Scribble Safari Necklace, 2003
1 ¾ x 20 ½ x 1 ¾" (4.4 x 52.1 x 4.4 cm)
Premo!, Liquid Sculpey; aluminum
armature, Bali silver beads
Photo by Steve Mann

WENDY WALLIN MALINOW

Box #8, 2000
6 ½ x 2 ½ x 2 ½" (16.5 x 6.3 x 6.3 cm)
Polymer clay; inlaid, carved
Photo by Courtney Frisse

CYNTHIA SEIWERT

Holiday Ornament, 2002
Largest 6 x 6 x 6" (15.2 x 15.2 x 15.2 cm)
Premo!; mouth-blown glass ball
Photo by Chuck May

I began to make these holiday ornaments when I realized
my beads had become too large to wear! —*CS*

JAY WHYTE

A Time For Healing, 2003
9 x 9" (22.9 x 22.9 cm)
Fimo; silver solder
Photo by artist

This bowl, with its vigorous silver fissures, cleverly
imitates lathe-turned wood and the Japanese
tradition of mending broken porcelain with a
precious-metal lacquer. —*ISD*

327

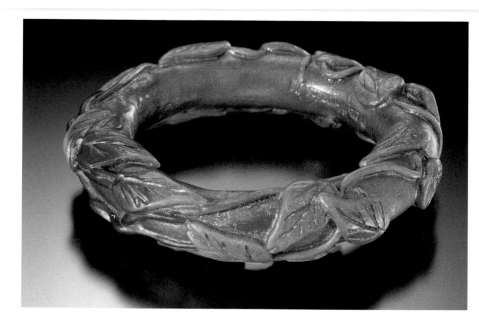

JILL ACKIRON-MOSES

Jade Bracelet, 2001
7 ¹/₂" (18.8 cm) diameter
Premo!; acrylic paint; carved
Photo by Hap Sakwa

ELLEN BERNE

Polymer Clay Chains, 2001
28" (71.1 cm)
Premo!; rolled, wrapped, sliced,
assembled, buffed
Photo by Barbara Hunt

These chains are made using traditional
metalsmithing techniques adapted to
polymer clay. The clay is hand rolled,
not extruded, so that it has greater
strength and durability. *−EB*

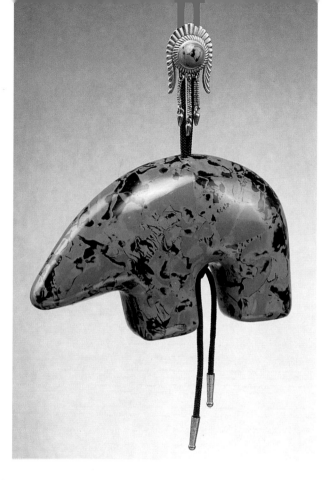

DIANE VILLANO

Big Bead–Zuni Turquoise Bear Fetish, 2001
4 ½ x 7 ¼ x 2 ¼" (11.4 x 17.8 x 5.7 cm)
Premo!; papier-mâché
Photo by William K. Sacco

ELISE WINTERS

Chrysalis Brooches, 2000
4 x ½ x ½" (10.2 x 1.3 x 1.3 cm)
Fimo, Premo!; crazed acrylic
Photo by Ralph Gabriner

DONNA BERRY

Fossil? (Beads), 2000
Largest 1 ½" (3.8 cm)
Fimo; acrylic paint
Photo by artist

My sculpture technique is based on play. Although
I have no final image in mind when I begin, I think
my prime influences are natural forms as seen
under a microscope, and my experience in
netsuke carving. —DB

GEORGIA MORGAN

Sword-Fitting Bracelet, 2003
1 ⅛ x 7 ¼ x ⅛" (3 x 18 x .4 cm)
Premo!, Fimo clay; gold-filled wire
Photo by Wilmer Zehr

MARGARET REGAN

Blue Cornucopia Bracelet, 2002
1 x 7 ¼ x 1" (2.5 x 18.1 x 2.5 cm)
Polymer clay; sterling silver, glass seed beads
Photo by Robert K. Liu/Ornament

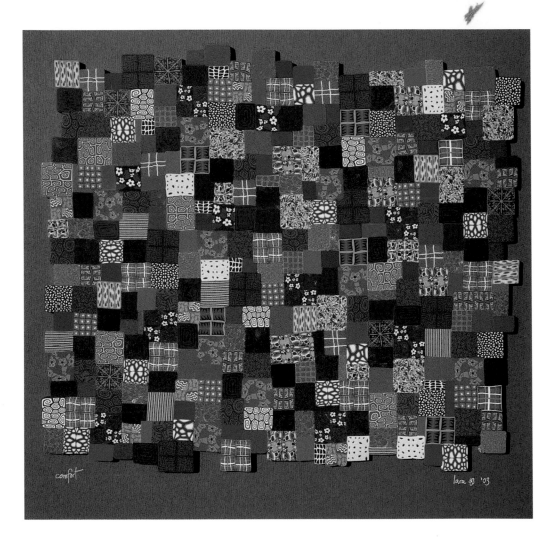

LARA MELNIK

Comfort, 2003
11 x 12" (27.9 x 30.5 cm)
Premo!; millefiori
Photo by Darren Holcombe

Caneworking, even in its simplest form, can be used in a
fresh and unusual way, as shown in this patchwork wall
piece. The variation in sizes of the "quilt blocks," as well
as the irregular edges of the piece, loosens its form. *–ISD*

HEN SCOTT

Verdigris Wild Boar Pot, 2003
3 x 3 x 3" (7.5 x 7.5 x 7.5 cm)
Premo!; textured, stamped
Photo by Archie Miles

KAREN MITCHELL

Mosaic Vest, 1997
16 x 13 x 8" (40.6 x 33 x 20.3 cm)
Premo!, Sculpey III; wire beading cord,
brass head pins, metallic glass beads,
fabric trim, glass cabochons, metallic leaf;
sculpted, cane veneers, mosaic, marbled
Photo by Steve Mann

This combines my education as a
costume designer with my professional
skills as a jewelry designer to create a
fitted, reversible garment made almost
entirely of clay. The entire piece was
constructed on a dress form to give the
vest its shape. *–KM*

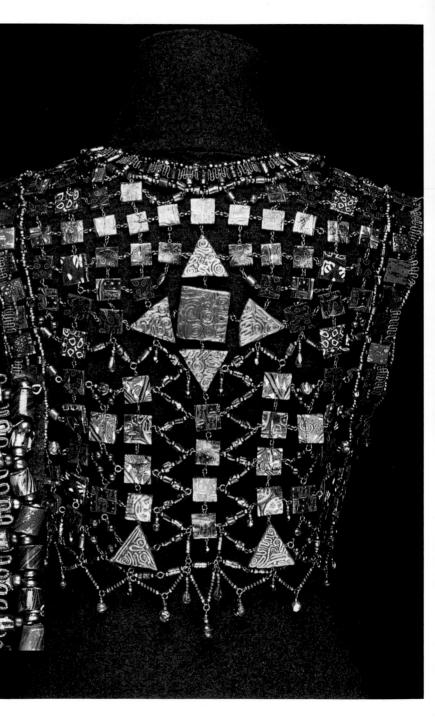

DAYLE DOROSHOW

Dreams of Italy, 2002
2 x 2 ½" (5.1 x 6.3 cm)
Fimo; photocopied and transferred
image, sewn hinge
Photo by Don Felton

MARY FILAPEK
LOU ANN TOWNSEND

Cluster of Will, 2003
7 x 5 ½ x ¼" (17.5 x 14 x .6 cm)
Polymer clay; sterling silver, stainless steel cable
Photo by Margot Geist

Irregular shapes and placement of the
"nuclei" give this piece lively energy.
Especially stimulating is the way the artists'
organic forms make negative space an
integral part of the design. –*ISD*

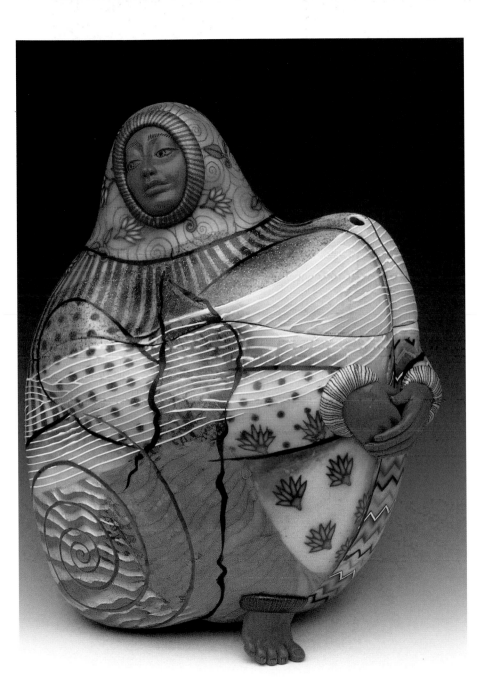

KATHLEEN DUSTIN

Village Woman Holding Knees–Purse, 1999
7 x 5 x 4" (17.5 x 12.7 x 10.2 cm)
Premo!, Sculpey III, liquid polymer; colored
pencil, gold leaf; layered, sanded, polished
Photo by George Post

KARYN KOZAK

Bottle, 2003
5 x 3 ½ x 1" (12.7 x 7.5 x 2.5 cm)
Fimo; porcelain armature; millefiori, sanded, polished
Photo by Ryell Ho

ACKNOWLEDGMENTS

Grateful thanks go to the many talented polymer clay artists who sent us slides of their beautiful creations. It is wonderful to see that this budding artistic medium has inspired so many. Their desire to promote appreciation of it is remarkable. We here at Lark are in awe of juror Irene Semanchuk Dean, whose indefatigable efforts have helped make polymer clay a household word; thank you so much for agreeing to be a part of this book. Sincere thanks must also go to Rosemary Kast and Nathalie Mornu, whose scrupulous work and cheerful demeanors make my work lighter and better; Delores Gosnell and Shannon Yokeley, who have perfect follow-through; and Jim Bixby of 828:design, who contributed his delightful creative talent to the art production of this lovely book.

Suzanne J.E. Tourtillott, Editor

INDEX